The Feast of Fools

A Theological Essay on Festivity and Fantasy

The Feast

A Theological Essay on Festivity

Harvard University Press

# of Fools

and Fantasy / by Harvey Cox

Cambridge, Massachusetts

© 1969 by Harvey Cox
All rights reserved
Second Printing, 1970
Library of Congress Catalog Card Number 75-95914
SBN 674-29525-0
Printed in the United States of America

To Rachel, Martin, and Sarah

Their irrepressible festivity and constant invitation to fantasy not only made this book possible but delightfully delayed its completion.

Preface

I wrote *The Feast of Fools* not to solve a scholarly problem, not even to advance any of the important technical discussions now going on in theology. I wrote it because I think what it says is true and is needed. In part, this book grows out of the thinking I have had to do in response to the criticisms that were made of *The Secular City*. Some people rightly saw that book as far too one-sided in its eager activism, its zealous concern for social change, its hyperthyroid extraversion. It was, in a way, a very "Protestant" book, at least in the Cal-vinistic-Puritan sense.

In this book I turn somewhat to the other side. If *The Secular City* was Apollonian, this book is more Dionysian, more playful, more generous to "religion" than was *The Secular City*. Some may even say it has more "soul." Without retreating from my affirmation of the secular, I touch here on a different range of issues, including meditation, mysticism, prayer, and ritual. I strongly emphasize the noninstrumental significance of celebration and liturgy. But I am not hereby revoking *The Secular City*. It bore on its original cover, after all, the slogan "A celebration of its liberties and an invitation to its disciplines." So my line of thinking here is not entirely unprecedented. I still stand by my basically positive estimate of the possibilities posed for us by pluralism and urban life. This book is intended as a companion piece to the earlier work, not as a recantation.

Still, I have changed some of my views in the five years since *The Secular City,* and not all these new insights have been entirely reconciled in my own mind. Politically, for example, I have become considerably more radical and would now place myself somewhere near the right fringe of the New Left, if such designations mean anything. I am hopeful in the long run about man's chances, but I see more clearly than I did five years ago that the changes we need are much more fundamental than I originally thought and that the method for achieving them must be much more drastic.

At the same time I have become aware that there is an unnecessary gap in today's world between the world-changers and the life-celebrators. One of the reasons why I wrote this book is because I want to see this gap closed. There is no reason why those who celebrate life cannot also be committed to fundamental social change. And world-changers need not be joyless and ascetic. St. Francis, the most life-affirming of the Christian saints, was a revolutionary at heart, and Karl Marx longed for a world in which work had become a kind of play. Ultimately radicals would be more effective if now and again they allowed themselves to live, if only on occasion, as though all the things that they were struggling for were already accomplished. Theologians might call this a kind of "proleptic liberation." It is happening already. The "festive radical" is appearing on the scene. Guerrilla theatre enlivens campus upheavals. Rock music is a staple among young activists. We may be witnessing the appearance of that mixture of "saint and revolutionary" Ignazio Silone said was needed to save our world from itself. This book is intended in part to help facilitate his appearance.

The core of this book consists of the ideas I marshalled for the William Belden Noble Lectures at Harvard University in the spring of 1968. I have, however, added a lot of material that was not included in the lectures and left out some that was in. I am sorry that because of the underdeveloped state of the publishing industry the slides, movies, music, balloons, and dancing that figured so prominently in the Noble Lectures themselves could not be included in this comparatively pale record of that polychromatic program.

Preface

I would like to thank all the people whose ideas and examples have enriched *The Feast of Fools*. My wife, Nancy, has learned to love and live with me despite my impulsive and unpredictable schedule as a writer and a theologian. My colleagues and students at Harvard University have kept me alive and humble. Two astonishingly competent and charming secretaries, Sharon Connelly and Mollie Babize, have typed and retyped sections of the manuscript. Ivan Illich and the students at the Center for Intercultural Documentation in Cuernavaca, Mexico, provided a festive input to my thinking during the summer of 1968. Mickey Myers and Steve Nelson not only lit up Memorial Church during the Noble Lectures, they also cheered and supported me during the arduous preparation. Friends and correspondents all over the world supplied ideas they will recognize, often without citation for they have become my own. I hope all these people like *The Feast of Fools*.

Harvey Cox

Roxbury, Massachusetts
May 1, 1969

Contents

Contents

Part Three

Overture & Introduction

Overture

During the medieval era there flourished in parts of Europe a holiday known as the Feast of Fools. On that colorful occasion, usually celebrated about January first, even ordinarily pious priests and serious townsfolk donned bawdy masks, sang outrageous ditties, and generally kept the whole world awake with revelry and satire. Minor clerics painted their faces, strutted about in the robes of their superiors, and mocked the stately rituals of church and court. Sometimes a Lord of Misrule, a Mock King, or a Boy Bishop was elected to preside over the events. In some places the Boy Bishop even celebrated a parody mass. During the Feast of Fools, no custom or convention was immune to ridicule and even the highest personages of the realm could expect to be lampooned.

The Feast of Fools was never popular with the higher-ups. It was constantly condemned and criticized. But despite the efforts of fidgety ecclesiastics and an outright condemnation by the Council of Basel in 1431, the Feast of Fools survived until the sixteenth century. Then in the age of Reformation and Counter-Reformation it gradually died out. Its faint shade still persists in the pranks and revelry of Halloween and New Year's Eve.

Chroniclers of Western history seldom lament the passing of the Feast of Fools. There are reasons why they do not. Often it did degenerate into debauchery and lewd buffoonery. Still, its death was a loss. The Feast of Fools had demonstrated that a culture could periodically make sport of its most sacred royal and religious practices. It could imagine, at least once in a while, a wholly different kind of world—one where the last was first, accepted values were inverted, fools became kings, and choirboys were prelates. The demise of the Feast of Fools signaled a significant change in the Western cultural mood: an enfeeblement of our civilization's capacity for festivity and fantasy. Its demise showed that people were beginning to see their social roles and sacred conventions through eyes that could not permit such strident satire, that they no longer had the time or the heart for such trenchant social parody.

Why did the Feast of Fools disappear? The question is part of a much larger one that scholars have debated for years. Are the religious patterns of postmedieval Europe the cause or the effect of the new social and economic practices that culminated in capitalism and the industrial revolution? Why did the virtues of sobriety, thrift, industry, and ambition gain such prominence at the expense of other values? Why did mirth, play, and festivity come in for such scathing criticism during the Protestant era?

I do not wish to join in that debate here. This is not a historical treatise and I recall the Feast of Fools only as a symbol of the subject of this book. It is important to notice however that festivity and fantasy do play a less central role among us now than they did in the days of holy fools, mystical visionaries, and a calendar full of festivals. And we are the poorer for it.

There are those who would claim that we still have festivity and fantasy, but that they take a different form. We celebrate at office parties, football games, and cocktail gatherings. Our fantasies glitter in the celluloid world of the cinema and on the pages of *Playboy*. Science fiction still conjures up fanciful worlds. Perhaps. But my contention in this book is that whatever forms of festivity and fantasy remain to us are shrunken and insulated. Our celebrations do not relate us, as they once did, to the parade of cosmic history or to the great stories of man's spiritual quest. Our fantasies tend to be cautious, eccentric, and secretive. When they do occasionally soar, they are appreciated only by an elite. Our feasting is sporadic or obsessive, our fantasies predictable and politically impotent. Neither provides the inspiration for genuine social transformation.

At least all of this has been true until quite recently. Now, however, we are witnessing a rebirth of the spirit of festivity and fantasy. Though we have no annual Feast of Fools, the life affirmation and playful irreverence once incarnated in that day are bubbling up again in our time. As expected, the bishops and the bosses are not happy about it, but it is happening anyway. This incipient renaissance of fantasy and festivity is a good sign. It shows that our period may be rediscovering the value of two components of culture both of which were once seen in the Feast of Fools. The first is the feast or festival itself: important because it puts work in its place. It suggests that work, however rewarding, is not the highest end of life but must contribute to personal human fulfillment. We need stated times for nonwork to remind us that not even an astronomical gross national product and total employment can bring a people salvation. On feast days we stop working and enjoy those traditional gestures and moments of human conviviality without which life would not be human. Festivity, like play, contemplation, and making love, is an end in itself. It is not instrumental.

The other important cultural component of the Feast of Fools is fantasy and social criticism. Unmasking the pretence of the powerful always makes their power seem less irresistible. That is why tyrants tremble before fools and dictators ban political cabarets. Though a stated occasion for political persiflage can be exploited by the powerful to trivialize criticism, it need not be. From the oppressor's point of view satire can always get out of hand or give people ideas, so it is better not to have it at all.

The Feast of Fools thus had an implicitly radical dimension. It exposed the arbitrary quality of social rank and enabled people to see that things need not always be as they are. Maybe that is why it made the power-wielders uncomfortable and eventually had to go. The divine right of kings, papal infallibility, and the modern totalitarian state all flowered after the Feast of Fools disappeared.

Today in the late twentieth century we need the spirit represented by the Feast of Fools. In a success- and money-oriented society, we need a rebirth of patently unproductive festivity and expressive celebration. In an age that has quarantined parody and separated politics from imagination we need more social fantasy. We need for our time and in our own cultural idiom a rediscovery of what was right and good about the Feast of Fools. We need a renaissance of the spirit, and there are signs that it is coming.

Introduction

I know nothing, except what everyone knows—
if there when Grace dances, I should dance.

—*W. H. Auden,* "Whitsunday in Kirchstetten"

Mankind has paid a frightful price for the present opulence of Western industrial society. Part of the price is exacted daily from the poor nations of the world whose fields and forests garnish our tables while we push their people further into poverty. Part is paid by the plundered poor who dwell within the gates of the rich nations without sharing in the plenty. But part of the price has been paid by affluent Western man himself. While gaining the whole world he has been losing his own soul. He has purchased prosperity at the cost of a staggering impoverishment of the vital elements of his life. These elements are *festivity*—the capacity for genuine revelry and joyous celebration, and *fantasy*—the faculty for envisioning radically alternative life situations.

Festivity and fantasy are not only worthwhile in themselves, they are absolutely vital to human life. They enable man to relate himself to the past and the future in ways that seem impossible for animals. The *festival,* the special time when ordinary chores are set aside while man celebrates some event, affirms the sheer goodness of what is, or observes the memory of a god or hero, is a distinctly human activity. It arises from man's peculiar power to incorporate into his own life the joys of other people and the experience of previous generations. Porpoises and chimpanzees may play. Only man celebrates. Festivity is a human form of play through which man appropriates an extended area of life, including the past, into his own experience.

Fantasy is also uniquely human. A hungry lion may dream about a zebra dinner but only man can mentally invent wholly new ways of living his life as an individual and as a species. If festivity enables man to enlarge his experience by reliving events of the past, fantasy is a form of play that extends the frontiers of the future.

Festivity, of course, does not focus solely on the past any more than fantasy reaches only toward the future. We also sometimes celebrate *coming* events, and our minds often re-create bygone experiences. But despite this obvious overlap, festivity is more closely related to memory, and fantasy is more akin to hope. Together they help make man a creature who sees himself with an origin and a destiny, not just as an ephemeral bubble.

Both our enjoyment of festivity and our capacity for fantasy have deteriorated in modern times. We still celebrate but our feasts and parties often lack real verve or feeling. Take for example a typical American New Year's Eve. It is a celebration, but there is something undeniably vacuous and frenetic about it. People seem anxiously, even obsessively determined to have a good time. Not to have a date for New Year's Eve is the ultimate adolescent tragedy. Even adults usually hate to spend the evening alone. On New Year's Eve we bring out the champagne and hurl paper streamers. But under the surface of Dionysiac carousing we feel something is missing. The next day we often wonder why we bothered.

Our mixed feelings about New Year's Eve reveal two things about us. First, we are still essentially festive and ritual creatures. Second, our contemporary feasts and rites are in a dismal state. The reason New Year's Eve is important is that it so vividly energizes both memory and hope. As hoping and remembering creatures, we rightly sense something of unusual symbolic significance about that peculiar magical time when the old year disappears forever and the new one begins. We personify the occasion with a bearded old man and a pink baby.

We take a cup of kindness for the past (for "old acquaint-
ance"), we kiss, we toast the future. The New Year's Eve party
demonstrates the vestigial survival of forgotten feasts and
rituals.

But the vaguely desperate air lurking behind the noisemakers
and funny hats is also significant. We dimly sense on New
Year's Eve and sometimes on other occasions a whole world
of empyrean ecstasy and fantastic hope, a world with which
we seem to have lost touch. Our sentimentality and wistfulness
arise from the fact that we have so few festivals left, and the
ones we have are so stunted in their ritual and celebrative
power.

Still, we are not wholly lost, and the fact that we still do ring
out the old and ring in the new reminds us that celebration,
however weakened, is not yet dead.

While festivity languishes, our fantasy life has also become
anemic. Once effulgent, it now ekes out a sparse and timid
existence. Our night dreams are quickly forgotten. Our daydreams are stealthy, clandestine, and unshared. Unable to
conjure up fantasy images on our own, we have given over the
field to mass production. Walt Disney and his imitators have
populated it with virtuous mice and friendly skunks. Low-
grade cinema and formula-TV producers have added banal
symbols and predictable situations. But the enfeeblement of
fantasy cannot be blamed on the mass media. It is the symptom
of a much larger cultural debility. Indeed, the sportive inventiveness of today's best filmmakers proves both that it is not
the technology which is at fault and that human fantasy still
survives in a dreary, fact-ridden world.

What are the reasons for the long, slow decay of festivity
and fantasy in the West? The sources of our sickness are complex. During the epoch of industrialization we grew more sober
and industrious, less playful and imaginative. Work schedules
squeezed festivity to a minimum. The habits formed are still
so much with us that we use our new technologically provided

leisure either to "moonlight," or to plan sober consultations on the "problem of leisure," or to wonder why we are not enjoying our "free time" the way we should.

The age of science and technology has also been hard on fantasy. We have J. R. R. Tolkien's hobbits and the visions of science fiction. But our fact-obsessed era has taught us to be cautious: always check impulsive visions against the hard data. Secularism erodes the religious metaphors within which fantasy can roam. Scientific method directs our attention away from the realm of fantasy and toward the manageable and the feasible. True, we are now discovering that science without hunches or visions gets nowhere, but we still live in a culture where fantasy is tolerated, not encouraged. Part of the blame belongs to secularism. There was a time when visionaries were canonized, and mystics were admired. Now they are studied, smiled at, perhaps even committed. All in all, fantasy is viewed with distrust in our time.

But why should we care if festivity and fantasy now play a smaller role in human life? Why not simply turn the world over to sobriety and rational calculation? Is anything significant lost? I believe that it is.

In the first place, the disappearance of festivity and fantasy simply makes life duller. They should be nurtured for their own sake. Further, man's very survival as a species has been placed in grave jeopardy by our repression of the human celebrative and imaginative faculties. I must also argue from theological premises that man will grasp his divine origin and destiny only if he regains the capacity for festive revelry and the ability to fantasize. Let me state these three theses as clearly as possible.

(1) Man is by his very nature a creature who not only works and thinks but who sings, dances, prays, tells stories, and celebrates. He is *homo festivus*. Notice the universal character of festivity in human life. No culture is without it. African pygmies and Australian primitives frolic in honor of the equi-

nox. Hindus revel at Holi. Moslems feast after the long fast of Ramadan. In some societies the principal festival comes at harvest or when the moon reaches a particular position. In others the anniversary of some event in the life of a cultural or religious hero supplies the cause for jubilation. There are important differences, as we shall mention later, between the cultures that stress cosmic or seasonal festivals and those that emphasize historical holidays, but all provide an occasion for singing old songs, saluting heroes, and reaffirming new and old aspirations. When festivity disappears from a culture something universally human is endangered.

Man is also *homo fantasia,* the visionary dreamer and myth-maker. If no culture is without some form of celebration, there is certainly none that lacks its share of wild and improbable stories. Fairies, goblins, giants, and elves—or their equivalent —inhabit the imagination of every race. Also, in most societies, one can find legends of a golden age in the past and, in some, stories of a wondrous age to come. Students of prehistoric man have often said more about man's tools than about his tales. Perhaps this derives from our present obsessive interest in technology. Perhaps it is because clubs and knives remain to be found, although myths disappear. Still, both were there very early and it was just as much his propensity to dream and fantasize as it was his augers and axes that first set man apart from the beasts.

Man is *homo festivus* and *homo fantasia.* No other creature we know of relives the legends of his forefathers, blows out candles on a birthday cake, or dresses up and pretends he is someone else.

But in recent centuries something has happened that has undercut man's capacity for festivity and fantasy. In Western civilization we have placed an enormous emphasis on man as worker (Luther and Marx) and man as thinker (Aquinas and Descartes). Man's celebrative and imaginative faculties have atrophied. This worker-thinker emphasis, enforced by industrialization, ratified by philosophy, and sanctified by Christianity, helped to produce the monumental achievements of Western science and industrial technology. Now, however, we can begin to see that our productivity has exacted a price. Not only have we gotten it at the expense of millions of other people in the poor nations, not only have we ruined countless rivers and lakes and poisoned our atmosphere, we have also terribly damaged the inner experience of Western man. We have pressed him so hard toward useful work and rational calculation he has all but forgotten the joy of ecstatic celebration, antic play, and free imagination. His shrunken psyche is just as much a victim of industrialization as were the bent bodies of those luckless children who were once confined to English factories from dawn to dusk.

Man is essentially festive and fanciful. To become fully human, Western industrial man, and his non-Western brothers insofar as they are touched by the same debilitation, must learn again to dance and to dream.

(2) The survival of mankind as a species has also been placed in jeopardy by the repression of festivity and fantasy. This is because man inhabits a world of constant change, and in such a world both festival and fantasy are indispensable for survival. If he is to survive man must be both innovative and adaptive. He must draw from the richest wealth of experience available to him and must never be bound to existing formulas for solving problems. Festivity, by breaking routine and opening man to the past, enlarges his experience and reduces his provincialism. Fantasy opens doors that merely empirical calculation ignores. It widens the possibilities for innovation. Together, festivity and fantasy enable man to experience his present in a richer, more joyful, and more creative way. Without them he may go the way of the diplodocus and the tyrannosaurus.

Psychiatrists remind us that the loss of a sense of time is a symptom of personal deterioration. Cut a man off from his memories or his visions and he sinks to a depressed state. The same is true for a civilization. So long as it can absorb what has happened to it and move confidently toward what is yet to come its vitality persists. But when a civilization becomes alienated from its past and cynical about its future, as Rome once did, its spiritual energy flags. It stumbles and declines.

Much has been written in recent years about man as a "historical" being, a spirit who perceives himself in time. These analyses have contributed much to our understanding of man. What they often overlook, however, is that our capacity to relate ourselves to time requires more than merely intellectual competence. Well-tabulated chronicles and sober planning alone do not keep us alive to time. We recall the past not only by recording it but by reliving it, by making present again its fears and delectations. We anticipate the future not only by preparing for it but by conjuring up and creating it. Our links to yesterday and tomorrow depend also on the aesthetic, emotional, and symbolic aspects of human life—on saga, play, and celebration. Without festivity and fantasy man would not really be a historical being at all.

In our present world it is also crucial for the rich Western nations to recover something of their capacity for sympathetic imagination and noninstrumental *joie de vivre* if they are to keep in touch with the so-called "underdeveloped world." Otherwise, the rich Western nations will become increasingly static and provincial or they will try to inflict their worship of work on the rest of the world. Unable to put themselves in someone else's shoes, they will grow more insensitive to the enclaves of poverty in their midst and the continents of hunger around them. Without relearning a measure of festivity on their own they will not be able to appreciate the gusto of Africa and Latin America. Deprived of joy they will become more hateful and suspicious toward "others." Without fantasy not even the radicals of the affluent world can identify with oppressed peoples in their battles for independence and national dignity. Without social imagination no one will be able to think up fundamentally new ways to relate to the rest of the world. Unless the industrialized world recovers its sense of festivity and fantasy, it will die or be destroyed.

(3) Our loss of the capacity for festivity and fantasy also has profound religious significance. The religious man is one who grasps his own life within a larger historical and cosmic setting. He sees himself as part of a greater whole, a longer story in which he plays a part. Song, ritual, and vision link a man to this story. They help him place himself somewhere between Eden and the Kingdom of God; they give him a past and a future. But without real festive occasions and without the nurture of fantasy man's spirit as well as his psyche shrinks. He becomes something less than man, a gnat with neither origin nor destiny.

This may account in part for the malaise and tedium of our time. Celebration requires a set of common memories and collective hopes. It requires, in short, what is usually thought of as a religion. For centuries Christianity provided our civilization with both the feast days that kept its history alive, and with the images of the future that sustained its expectations. Stories of Adam, Noah, and Abraham rooted us in the recesses of our prehistory. The saints supplied images of human perfection. The Kingdom of God and the New Jerusalem with their visions of peace and social fulfillment kept us hopeful about the future. At Christmas and Easter, and to some extent during the other holy days, the figure of Jesus somehow enlivened both our primal memories and our wildest hopes. The last of the prophets of Israel, Jesus was also seen as the first citizen of an epoch still to be fulfilled. Thus did Western man, richly supplied with cultural memories and vivid aspirations, once celebrate his place in history and in the cosmos.

Today, however, something seems to be wrong. Our feast days have lost their vitality. Christmas is now largely a family reunion, Easter a spring style show, and on Thanksgiving there is no one to thank. The potency has drained from the religious symbols that once kept us in touch with our forebears. The images that fired our hopes for the future have lost their glow. We often see the past as a cage from which we must escape, and the future as a dull elongation of what we now have. Without a past that is somehow truly our own, and devoid of a really engaging vision of the future, Western man today either frets in a dreary present with no exit or spends himself in the frenzied pursuit of goals that turn to ashes in his grasp.

The blame for this state of affairs is usually placed on the thinkers and seers of Christianity themselves. Challenged by modern science, industrialization, pluralism, and secularization, they have not yet accomplished the badly needed intellectual reformation of the faith. This is true as far as it goes. But there is another side to the story too. Christianity has often adjusted too quickly to the categories of modernity. It has speeded industrialization by emphasizing man as the soberly responsible worker and husbandman. It has nourished science by stressing the order of creation and the gift of reason. In fact, without Protestant ethics and medieval scholasticism, our scientific civilization might never have developed. Christianity has recognized that man is the worker and toolmaker, the reasoner and thinker. But in doing all this, it has often failed to give sufficient attention to vital dimensions of the human reality, some of which are more clearly seen by other religious traditions. Consequently Western Christian culture, though we rightly speak of it as "highly developed" in some senses, is woefully underdeveloped in others. It has produced too many pedestrian personalities whose capacity for vision and ecstasy is sadly crippled. It has resulted in a deformed man whose sense of a mysterious origin and cosmic destiny has nearly disappeared. A race that has lost touch with past and future through the debilitation of ritual, revelry, and visionary aspirations will soon shrink to a tribe of automatons. Machines, as we know, can be astonishingly efficient. But there are some things they cannot do. Among other things they cannot really play, pretend, or prevaricate. They cannot frolic or fantasize. These activities are somehow uniquely human and if they vanish man loses essential reminders of his singularity.

It is important to emphasize that among other things man in his very essence is *homo festivus* and *homo fantasia*. Celebrating and imagining are integral parts of his humanity. But Western industrial man in the past few centuries has begun to lose his capacity for festivity and fantasy, and this loss is calamitous for three reasons: (1) it deforms man by depriving him of an essential ingredient in human existence, (2) it endangers his very survival as a species by rendering him provincial and less adaptive, and (3) it robs him of a crucial means of sensing his important place in fulfilling the destiny of the cosmos. The loss is personal, social, and religious.

The picture, however, is not quite as bleak as I have painted it so far. Despite the long-term erosion, it is also true that in very recent years, industrial man has begun to rediscover the festive and the fanciful dimensions of life. A centuries-long process may be reversing itself. Our recent increased exposure both to non-Western cultures and to those sectors of our own civilization that have escaped complete integration into the industrialization process have made us aware that we are missing something. Technologically produced leisure has forced us to ask ourselves some hard questions about our traditional worship of work. Young people in industrial societies everywhere are demonstrating that expressive play and artistic creation belong in the center of life, not at its far periphery. A theatre of the body replete with mime, dance, and acrobatics is upstaging our inherited theatre of the mind. Street festivals, once disappearing as fast as the whooping crane, are coming back. Psychiatrists and educators are beginning to reject their traditional roles as the punishers of fantasy. Some are even searching for ways to encourage it. The awakened interest of white people in the black experience has enhanced our appreciation for a more festive and feeling-oriented approach to life. We call it "soul." Films, novels, and plays explore the world of dreams and even some philosophers are rediscovering the significance of fantasy. Even in the churches, dance, color, movement, and new kinds of music dramatize the recovery of celebration. In short we may be witnessing the overture to a sweeping cultural renaissance, a revolution of human sensibilities in which the faculties we have starved and repressed during the centuries of industrialization will be nourished and appreciated again.

But it could turn out differently. What we take as the evidence of a cultural rebirth in our midst may be a deceptive flush on the cheek of a dying age. Or, an equally grim prospect, the hesitant beginnings of a festive resurrection in our time could be smashed or spoiled. Still worse, the present rebirth of spontaneous celebration and unfettered imagining could veer off into destructive excess or vacuous frivolity.

Which of these things will happen? We do not know. In fact the fate of our embryonic cultural revolution is still open and undecided. What will happen to it is largely up to us. The purpose of this book is to examine both the loss and the re-emergence of festivity and fantasy in our civilization, and to evaluate both processes from a theological perspective. I do not labor under the delusion that theology can either spark or stave off a cultural revolution in our time. It may play a role in the eventual outcome but its role will probably be a minor one. Nevertheless, theology has a deep stake in the outcome of our crisis not just because it is committed to man but also because the crisis is in part a religious one. If twentieth-century man finally succumbs and does lose the last remnants of his faculties for festivity and fantasy, the result will be disastrous. The heart of the religious view of man and the cosmos, especially in its Christian version, will be torn out. Correspondingly, if the battle for man's humanity is to be won at all, a religious vision will have to play an important role in that victory.

Ironically, the contemporary religious views of man, whether that of Teilhard de Chardin, of Martin Buber, or of Jürgen Moltmann, now face a criticism that is nearly the opposite of the one theologians faced two centuries ago. At that time the typical enlightened critique alleged that Christianity belittled man, called him a "despicable worm" or a "worthless sinner," when it was clear, at least to the critics, that man was really a noble and elevated being. A certain type of humanism emerged in conscious opposition to Christianity. Today the shoe is often on the other foot. Secular critics of Christianity find religion unreasonably affirmative in its estimate of man's place. Against what seems to be Christianity's groundlessly grandiose view of human destiny, the secularist frequently reminds us that we are, after all, only a transient eczema on a small planet in a third-rate galaxy. Its critics now often deride Christianity not for making man paranoid but for giving him what seem to be illusions of grandeur.

The fact that the continuing debate between religious and nonreligious intellectuals has recently taken this turn is a significant one. It means that the stature and significance of man rather than the existence of the deity is now the main focus of discussion. It also suggests that religion's stake in the rebirth of festivity and fantasy is even deeper than we had at first supposed. Festival occasions enlarge enormously the scope and intensity of man's relation to the past. They elevate his sense of personal worth by making him a part of an epic. Fantasy offers an endless range of future permutations. It inevitably escalates man's sense of his powers and possibilities. Therefore, the cultivation of celebration and imagination is crucial to religion and to man himself, if the biblical estimate of his status ("a little lower than the angels") has any validity. Perhaps this is why observance and revelry, ritual and myth have nearly always been central to religion, and why they seem to be making a comeback today.

Part One

Festivity: The Ingredients

1

Midnight too is noon; pain too is a joy; curses too are a blessing; night too is a sun—go away or you will learn: a sage too is a fool . . . Have you ever said Yes to a single joy? O my friends, then you said Yes too to all *woe.*

—*Friedrich Nietzsche,* Thus Spake Zarathustra

Rejoice in the Lord, O you righteous!
Praise befits the upright.
Praise the Lord with the lyre,
  make melody to him with the harp of ten strings!
Sing to him a new song,
  play skilfully on the strings, with loud shouts.

—*Psalm 33:1-3 (RSV)*

We begin with festivity, not an easy term to define. It is something we all enjoy but rarely think about. Furthermore, it is hard to be festive and to think about it at the same time. Celebration demands a kind of unselfconscious participation that prevents our analyzing it while it is happening. If we begin analyzing our experience of festivity during a celebration we stop celebrating—and the object of our examination vanishes. If we try to analyze it at another time, we can do so only through memory or anticipation. If we try to scrutinize someone else's festivity, we can never be sure we know what he is feeling, and we may even dampen his spirit. No one welcomes the guest who dissects the party while it is still in progress, or observes the mourners without himself shedding a tear.

Still some excellent analyses have been done of festivity as a human phenomenon. The French philosopher Roger Caillois believes that festivity is mainly marked by a resurgence of excess and chaos.[1] He sees it as a kind of social paroxysm in which the more instinctive and disorderly components of human life are temporarily allowed to express themselves. He has a point. Anyone who has roamed the Left Bank of Paris on Bastille Day, attended a cast party on the closing night of a play, seen a tribal fertility orgy, or imbibed the frenzied air at the victorious end of a war would tend to agree with Caillois. A certain contagion of excess does seem to characterize festivity, but there are also other ingredients.

Josef Pieper, in his book *In Tune With the World: A Theory of Festivity,* calls attention to the elements of rejoicing and affirmation in festivity. He also dwells on the fact that festivity is an activity pursued for its own sake. To celebrate for Pieper is to live out "the universal assent to the world as a whole." [2] A festival for Pieper is a special time in which we affirm *all* of life by saying a joyous *yes* to part of it. He reminds us of Nietzsche's famous aphorism, "If it be granted that we say Yea to a single moment, then in so doing we have said Yea not only to ourselves, but to all existence." [3] Other writers such as Gerardus van der Leeuw emphasize the religious and ritual sources of festivity,[4] or, as Johan Huizinga in *Homo Ludens* (Man Playing) discuss festivity as a form of play.[5]

Each of these discussions contains an element of truth, for festivity is a more complex reality than we sometimes imagine. For our purposes here, drawing in part on the work of these writers, I want to define festivity first of all as a socially approved occasion for the expression of feelings that are normally repressed or neglected. But just what sort of occasion is it? A festive occasion has three essential ingredients: (1) conscious excess, (2) celebrative affirmation, and (3) juxtaposition.

(1) By *excess* I mean that festive activity is revelry. We always "overdo it," and we do so on purpose. We "live it up." We stay up later, eat and drink more, and spend more money than we ordinarily would. Perhaps we laugh or cry or both. In

some cultures conventional sexual mores and food taboos are temporarily relaxed. For a festive occasion we "dress up"—and the phrase is instructive. Sometimes we wear things that would be stared at curiously or disapprovingly on most occasions: funny hats, tuxedos, daring dresses, exotic shirts; in some circles, even rows of medals and crimson sashes. We clothe ourselves, that is, with calculated excess. Festivity provides a short vacation from convention, and without elements of socially approved infraction of the norms of ordinary behavior, festivity would not be festivity.

(2) By *celebrative affirmation,* I mean that festivity always entails "saying yes to life." It includes joy in the deepest sense. It may be affirmation *because of* something that has happened, like a new job or a diploma, or it may celebrate something that is still only hoped for. It may even be celebration that occurs partly *in spite* of something that has happened. Think of the furious jigs at the old Irish wakes, or Zorba's fiery dance after the spectacular collapse of the slide in the movie *Zorba the Greek.* At such times we affirm life and gaiety despite the facts of failure and death.

(3) *Juxtaposition* is related to the element of excess. It means simply that festivity must display contrast. It must be noticeably different from "everyday life." In one of his songs Pete Seeger used to ask why we could not have Christmas the whole year round. But we know we cannot. Part of the appeal of Christmas comes because it does occur only once a year. It is appropriate that holidays are printed in red on the calendar. Festivity, however, cannot be reduced merely to the unusual. It is not *just* not working; it includes celebration and excess as we have mentioned. But the reality of festivity depends on an alternation with the everyday schedule of work, convention, and moderation. As Josef Pieper says: "The festive quality of a holiday depends on its being exceptional." [6]

These three elements of festivity help us to keep alive to time by relating past, present, and future to each other. The first element, *excess,* for example, shows our willingness to suspend on occasion our habitual Western derogation of the present as mere preparation for the future. A festival embraces the moment. Says Pieper: "It is in no way tied to other goals, it has been removed from all 'so that' and 'in order to.' " [7] In festive excess we delight in the here and now, putting out of our minds for the moment the fact that we have to get up for work tomorrow or that we may be overtaxing our legs or our digestive tract.

Celebration links us both to past and to future, but the emphasis varies depending on what we are celebrating. A saint's day in a Mexican village revives for a time the piety and exploits of the holy one. A wedding feast or a *bar mitzvah* expresses our hopes for the future. Celebration thus helps us affirm dimensions of time we might ordinarily fear, ignore, or deny.

Finally, *juxtaposition,* the third element in festivity, makes us more conscious of the continuity of history by allowing us to step back from it temporarily. It provides a contrast, a Copernican point where we can stand while we hold the workaday environment temporarily at bay. In this way the world we hardly see because we are so absorbed in it periodically becomes visible.

Festivity then is a time set aside for the full expression of feeling. It consists of an irreducible element of prodigality, of "living it up." It says yes to experience; it entails joy, which explains why we wish people happiness on holidays and consider a party successful if "a good time was had by all." Festivity, as something we do for its own sake, provides us with a short vacation from the daily round, an alternation without which life would be unbearable. In addition, there are some things festivity is not.

(1) *Festivity is not superficiality.* It recognizes tragedy. This may help to explain the marked contrast between the lack of real festivity in most middle-class American religion on the

one hand and the ebullience of some forms of Latin Catholicism. The latter is festive not because it ignores or represses the evil side of life, but precisely because it recognizes and even affirms it. As F. S. C. Northrop points out: "At no point do the values of the Indian and the Spanish spirit stand in greater contrast to those of the Anglo-American people to their north . . ." than in the conviction of Spanish Americans "that tragedy, brutality, chaos, failure, and death, as well as triumph and compassion, aim at order, and earthly life are an essential part of the glory of man." [8] In observing the religion of the poor and the black in America it is clear that the ability to celebrate with real abandon is most often found among people who are no strangers to pain and oppression.

All this suggests that real celebration, rather than a retreat from the reality of injustice and evil, occurs most authentically where these negative realities are recognized and tackled, not where they are avoided. An antiseptic religion shies away from guilt and terror as well as eros and mirth. Its world becomes flat and anemic. "Imagine," Northrop asks, "how the Protestant religion must appear to the religious Mexicans. Its exceedingly verbal preaching, its aesthetic color-blindness, and its emotional tepidity and coldness must make it look to them like no religion at all." [9] Black Americans often have a similar view of the white churches of America—tepid, colorless, overly formal, and bland. The revivalist side of American religious history once gave a real place to emotion and feeling in religion. But since the second "Great Awakening" petered out about 1850, most of American Protestantism has emphasized moral earnestness, doctrinal clarity, and intellectual rigor, even when it has failed to attain any of them. Perhaps what conventional Protestants have to gain today from the more intuitively oriented religious groups is an occasional tongue of fire.

(2) *Also, festivity is not frivolity.* The two are radically different though on the surface they may occasionally appear to be similar. In his famous essay "On Frivolity," Jean Cocteau

sees the destructive possibilities in the kind of fantasy that springs from a frivolous rather than a celebrative spirit.[10] Such frivolous fantasy, Cocteau says, is really incapable of originality. It wants only to astonish and catch the eye. It manages to communicate to us an attitude of condescension for what it assumes is our stupid conventionality. Frivolity is the painted smile on a terminally sick patient. Its waggishness springs not from a joyous confidence in the ultimate goodness of life but from a despairing failure to make any sense out of it.

Cynical frivolity and confident play are similar only on the surface. Underneath they depend on utterly disparate views of the world. There is another kind of frivolousness, however, and Cocteau is aware of that too. It is the frivolousness of taking oneself and one's effort too seriously. Cocteau says he accuses of frivolity "any person capable of trying to solve problems of local interest without the least sense of absurdity." [11] The sense of absurdity called for here has nothing to do with nihilism. It is not some final absurdity of the universe that we must recognize; it is the relative absurdity of our efforts, something we can accept without ceasing to make the effort. This links festivity to play and to the comic sensibility that is so close to Christianity, as we shall show later on.

Festivity, with its essential ingredients—excess, celebration, and juxtaposition—is itself an essential ingredient in human life. Its loss severs man's roots in the past and clips back his reach toward the future. It dulls his psychic and spiritual sensibilities. For this reason it should not surprise us that the spiritual phenomenon we call the "death of God" should have happened in Western industrial society, that place on the globe where festivity has reached its lowest ebb. Nor is it a coincidence that Nietzsche, the same philosopher who deplored the disappearance of festivity in Christendom, also gave the phrase "God is dead" its first wide hearing. The link between the decline of festivity and the death of God can be fully substantiated.

Festivity and the Death of God 2

On the willows there
we hung up our lyres.
For there our captors
required of us songs,
and our tormentors, mirth, saying
"Sing us one of the songs of Zion!"
How shall we sing the Lord's song
in a foreign land?

—*Psalm 137: 2-4 (RSV)*

The Demise of Deity

Only, where are they? the flowers, the familiar,
the crowns of the feast-day?
...Why no more does a god mark a mortal man's
forehead ...

—*Friedrich Hölderlin,* Bread and Wine

The epochal crisis of Western consciousness which we call the death of God is not just a passing fad. It is the result of a cumulative history that includes industrialization and the ascent of technology, pluralism, modern science, and cultural self-consciousness. Most importantly, however, the vivid cultural experience of God's absence, disappearance, or death occurred in a civilization where festivity in all its forms was in a state of steady decline.

The death of God cannot be repealed, but it can be transcended. Theologically speaking it is a crisis that is deeply related to our distorted Western attitude toward history and history-making. Since celebration is what restores us to a proper view of history-making, an understanding of celebration may provide us with a useful clue to finding our way forward. We must see that the problem of the death of God is not merely an intellectual one. It is also intuitive and aesthetic. Men today do not simply complain that they cannot believe in God on intellectual grounds. Indeed a religious explanation of the universe may be just as conceptually adequate as another one. That is not the problem. The problem is that people do not "experience" or "encounter" God. Religious language including the word "God" will make sense again only when the lost experiences to which such words point become a felt part of the human reality. If God returns we may have to meet him first in the dance before we can define him in the doctrine.

Men are historical. Not only are they born and do they die; they know it. And so do civilizations. They both live in history. They both live in a world created by human meanings and intentions. But both men and civilizations shade off at their beginnings and their ends into something other than history. The rise of a civilization and the birth of a child both remind us of the mystery that still shrouds the sources of biological life and cultural meaning. Individual death and the demise of a whole civilization remind us of the larger and more inclusive reality that encompasses history.

"History" is the name we as human beings give to the horizon of consciousness within which we live. This historical horizon is surrounded, however, by a larger environment whose contours are harder to discern and whose name is less definite. Mircea Eliade calls it "cosmos";[1] Teilhard de Chardin named it the "divine milieu."[2] Intuition, ecstasy, and awe open us to this larger cosmic circle. Idea, analysis, and conscious decision relate us to the smaller historical one. Our religious symbols help us link the one to the other. History is defined by time, the cosmic circle suggests eternity. To be fully human we need to be in touch with both. As T. S. Eliot says in the *Four Quartets:*

But to apprehend
The point of intersection of the timeless
With time, is an occupation for the saint—
No occupation either, but something given
And taken, in a lifetime's death in love,
Ardour and selflessness and self-surrender.[3]

Our present religious crisis, especially in the Western world, stems from the loss of the critical "point of intersection" that kept us in touch with both these worlds. Some have referred to this loss as the death of God. The phrase, though hardly a new one in our time, is still apt. It conveys the fact that for many people the loss seems irrevocable, and in one sense it is. In another way, however, the loss is not final. It dramatizes the failure of our present religious symbols and ideas to provide any access to Eliot's point of intersection. The problem lies not in the stars, and not with God, but with ourselves.

In the past religions have provided the means by which man kept in symbolic touch both with history and with the divine milieu, history's larger environment. The trouble is that most religions have done the one at the expense of the other. We sometimes speak of "archaic" or "nonhistorical" religions on the one hand in contrast to "historical" religions on the other. Tibetan Buddhism and the religion of the ancient Mayans are examples of the first. Christianity and Islam are examples of the second. The contrast can be overdrawn for most religions are mixtures. Still the foci of religious traditions vary widely. The archaic, cosmic religions center on the recurrent funda-mentals of life and nature—the wheeling stars, the changing seasons, birth, sex, death. They help man situate himself in the larger cosmic setting of which he is undeniably a part. But they do not encourage him to be a history-maker.

The more historical faiths, on the other hand, spring from particular events—the exodus from Egypt, Mohammed's flight from Mecca, the crucifixion of Christ. Understandably, the historical religions have produced a mentality that takes historical events and the possibilities of human history-making very seriously. This is one reason why our Western festivals, both religious and secular, usually celebrate historical events and persons—the birth of Jesus, the fall of the Bastille, the Declaration of Independence, the desperate revolt of the Maccabean Jews, the deaths of soldiers, the struggle of the labor movement. It also accounts for our enormous self-consciousness about history and the vast importance we attach to it.

But it is just this preoccupation with history, some say today, that is at the very root of our crisis. Having learned the importance of history from our religion, we have now lost our religion and are left only with history. Because God seems gone we have lost sight of history's "divine milieu" and, therefore, we spoil history by overloading it with too much attention and expectation. Richard Rubenstein, for example, argues eloquently in *After Auschwitz* that this overloading of historical expectation is just what is destroying us, and he puts the finger on Western religion as the culprit that has misled us.[4] God placed the knife at his own throat. By keeping us constantly focused on history, Rubenstein contends, Western religions trap us into endless false expectations and thus into paroxysms of guilt. This cycle of titanism and failure, says Rubenstein, not only creates its own need for a forgiving God but also pushes us to desperate attempts to "solve" things and to kill God or anyone else when he gets in our way. For Rubenstein it is no accident that the stench of Auschwitz, the "final solution," arose from the soil of a Western "Christian" nation, and has thrust the whole West into an unprecedented seizure of guilt, rationalization, and evasion. The ovens, says Rubenstein, are the logical outcome of Western man's preoccupation with solving all the problems of history.

In place of all this Rubenstein urges a religion that extols the great constants of life: love, suffering, death. He rejects the God of history and advocates a gentle paganism, a veneration of soil, earth, and fertility. He would have us build temples and holy places to draw us away from the madding crowd of social change and to help us quietly regain our psychic humility and our bearings.[5]

Rubenstein's case is a persuasive one, in part because everyone knows in his own experience today how desperately harried our age has become. We know in our nerve cells as we rush from appointment to appointment that something is badly out of kilter. We feel responsible for so much that a certain desperation has begun to set in. Sensing our plight, we now listen to widely disparate voices commending a radically different life style—voices we would have refused even to hear only a short time back. This explains in part the impact of Norman O. Brown.

Brown insists that history itself is a cruel burden of repression.[6] Beginning with Freud's view that repression is the price we pay for civilization, Brown does to Freud what Marx did to Hegel—he turns him upside down, or as Brown would claim, right side up. He declares that the price is too high. He wants to get away from repressive historical consciousness so that man can "be ready to live instead of making history, to enjoy instead of paying back old scores and debts, and to enter that state of Being which was the goal of his Becoming."[7] History for Brown is not just one damned thing after another, it is all one big mistake.

We have come a long way from the nineteenth century. In those halcyon days man killed God in order to take over history.

Now we have history on our hands and we do not like it. In France popularized versions of the thought of Claude Lévi-Strauss and the other structuralists suggest that we are all pathologically overcommited to decision-making, temporal aims, and historical objectives. History must be "cooled down" and our anxious interest in its outcome qualified. Sartre, the philosopher of free decision and human world-making must be left behind, Lévi-Strauss argues, as the last of the nineteenth-century thinkers.

Like the song of the sirens, the call away from history-making is dulcet and tempting, but it could lure us onto the rocks. It is not an invitation we can or should accept. Still, the insistence that we are overly fixated on history is probably all too true, and the challenge to us to cool down this consciousness is correct. But how?

Our century has so far produced two answers to this question. One is to erase man's sense of himself as a historical being simply by eradicating the past. As the early surrealists said, "Burn the Louvre!" Some advocates of this position want to expunge the past in the interests of the present, others for the benefit of the future. Both want to make man "ahistorical" by excising memory and starting all over. There is another answer, however. There is a festive way of appropriating the past, a way that accepts the past without being bound by it, that views past history not as a prison to escape or as an antique to be preserved but as a dimension of reality that enlarges and illuminates the present.

I favor the second way. In my opinion the wanton destruction of the past will not revive a dead God or bring new life to man. It will only worsen the problem. Christianity's traditional fixation on the past will not help either. What is needed is a way of helping man to embrace his past with joy and to appreciate both history and its limits. This will happen only when we learn again to celebrate, to affirm both life and history without being suffocated by them.

The Immolation of the Past

. . . our veneration for what has already been created,
however beautiful and valid it may be, petrifies us . . .

—*Antonin Artaud,* The Theatre and Its Double

Man has tried in previous periods of history to sever his connections with the past. Such periods, however, have generally called for the reconstruction of a lost golden age, an Arcadian "natural" period before priests and kings spoiled things. Our period harks back to no lost Eden. It is in revolt against the very idea of historical continuity itself. Recently the well-known historian Lynn White, Jr., wrote that "our inherited intellectual processes, emotional attitudes and vocabulary are no longer of much use for analyzing and interpreting the spiritual revolution going on all around us." [8] Although we have all heard sentiments like this before, mainly from young artists and activists, it comes as a shock to realize that the man who uttered them is a distinguished scholar whose field is not cybernetics or psychedelics but medieval history. For White, to think in continuity with the great Western tradition not only does not help us today, it incapacitates us. "The new world in which we live is so unlike the past, even the past that is close to us, that in proportion as we are saturated in the Western cultural tradition we are incapacitated for looking clearly at our actual situation and thinking constructively about it. The better we are educated, the more we are fitted to live in a world that no longer exists." [9]

Another historian, this time Hayden V. White, reminds us that a good deal of modern fiction focuses on the attempt to liberate Western man from the "tyranny of the historical consciousness." Such literature insists that it is only by disenthralling human intelligence from the sense of history that men will be able to confront creatively the problems of the present."

White says that any historian today must ask himself how he can participate in this liberating activity and whether his participation "entails the destruction of history itself." [10]

When historians see the Western cultural tradition as incapacitating, and the task of the historian as "the destruction of history," something has gone wrong with our feeling for the past.

There was a time when traditional status endowed an idea with a certain authority. Then came a time in which mere continuity with the past no longer established the truth or worth of anything. The past competed on an equal basis with the present. Today we are developing an active prejudice against the past. Increasingly the fact that something has been done or said before not only does not establish its validity but even argues against it. Large numbers of people today, some of them the taste-makers of our time, instinctively distrust the artistic masterpiece, the classical virtue, the established fact, the historical doctrine. The past is in disrepute.

Furthermore, our present negative attitude toward the past displays an unprecedented intensity. It has the quality of an immolation. We consciously sacrifice it in order to gain something of greater value. Like Savonarola smashing the artistic creations of Florence or Luther burning the Papal Bull, we set the torch to the past because we believe it is somehow an obstacle to our secular salvation. As we examine this hostility toward the past we shall see that it is widespread but not monolithic. It appears in at least two different modes.

The first opposes the past mainly because the past is believed to prevent us from expecting or creating a new future. I shall call it "eschatological" immolation because it derogates both past and present in the name of the future. In its cultural aspect it becomes most explicit in the ideas of the late French theatrical writer Antonin Artaud.

The second opposes the past not because it has any real hope for the future but because it believes the past prevents us from enjoying the present. I call this "incarnational" immolation because it focuses so emphatically on what *is* instead of on what was or what could be. It can be seen in connection with the *avant-garde* composer John Cage.

Eschatological Immolation

Antonin Artaud is important not just because he typifies so much of today's total contempt for the past but also because his ideas have become so influential in the contemporary theatre, even among people who have never read him.[11]

Though he never claimed to be a Christian, Artaud had a vision of life and of art that he admitted was pervasively religious. Jean-Louis Barrault called him "the metaphysician of the theatre." Artaud insisted in his various manifestos that Western theatre had been off the track for centuries and should now seek to become a caldron of magic, violence, and extreme action. The now muted and stupefied audience should no longer be allowed to sit as mere spectators. They should be seduced, attacked, or assaulted into response and participation. Artaud is the originator of the "theatre of cruelty" by which he meant not just that the theatre should depict violence, although he did not exclude that either, but that it should deal in the raw, abrasive aspects of existence. His spirit can be seen in the Beck-Malina "Living Theatre" in which actors often harass and insult the patrons. It appears in the plays of Jean Genêt (*The Blacks*), Peter Weiss (*Marat/Sade*), and Boris Vian (*The Empire Builders*). It also comes to us in many elements of modern cinema and television, though Artaud himself disliked the film.

In one of his most famous essays, Artaud says: "One of the reasons for the asphyxiating atmosphere in which we live . . . is our respect for what has been written, formulated or painted, what has been given form, as if all expression were not at last exhausted, were not at a point where things must break apart if they are to start anew and begin afresh." Masterpieces of the past, Artaud insists, "are good for the past: they are not good for us." We must say what is vital to us, whether or not it has been said in the past, in a way that is "immediate and direct, corresponding to present modes of feeling, and understandable to everyone." Artaud wanted the theatre to get away from the mere *examination* of how hatred, pain, ambition, jealousy, and fear of fate operate in the lives of particular characters on stage. He wanted theatre to *propel* the spectators themselves into a direct and even terrifying encounter with these forces. Real theatre, he said, should leave the public with "an ineffable scar." [12]

For Artaud, a direct experience of the present is only spoiled by reliance on the past. But he went further. Even the present was not enough. Theatre should propel man into fantasy and dreaming. Artaud hoped for the appearance of what he called "a religious idea of the theatre," one which would enable us to "recover within ourselves those energies which ultimately *create* order and *increase* the value of life." [13] As he lit the faggots for the immolation, Artaud argued that the greatest obstacles between us and such a theatre of magic and religion is our "superstitious valuation of the past." His was a religion of mystery and incantation, of the marvelous and the disastrous. He believed in a power beyond human life but also believed that "our veneration for what has already been created, however beautiful and valid it may be, petrifies us, deadens our responses, and prevents us from making contact with that underlying power." [14]

For Artaud, man must destroy the past in order to create the future. Though he never used the word, his vision of theatre was "eschatological." Theatre should cease trying to convey ideas and should become an alembic of creativity. It should turn from moralizing and begin initiating man into a new reality. Lights should be selected not to enhance the play but to blister the eyes of the audience. Movements should be elemental and words should be selected not first for their idea content but for their "vibration," the sound and emotional resonance they exude. All this was designed to release man from the grip of the past and stir him into life and creation.

With the possible exception of Bertolt Brecht, no one has influenced the modern theatre more than Antonin Artaud. Since theatre both forms and reflects the sensibility of an era, anyone who wishes to speak to our time must understand the full portent of his thesis: the continuation or replication of the past, however well done, is an abdication from life. Reality must be conjured up through incantation and curse. Past must be exorcised. "What has been done" is viewed as an obstacle to human fulfillment, a barrier to be demolished. History is immolated in the name of the future.

Incarnational Immolation

This same compulsion to escape from the claws of continuity is also evident in the writing and music of John Cage, perhaps the most self-conscious *avant-gardist* of American music. Cage, like Artaud, has set himself against the whole Western tradition, this time not of theatre but of musical composition. But Cage's opposition to the past is incarnational, not eschatological. He opposes it not in the name of the future but for the sake of a world that is already here to savor and enjoy. For this reason, Cage fears that when music is "composed," those who hear it performed do not really listen to the sound itself but try to listen *through* the sound to the intention of the composer. Sound, which has a value and a fascination in its own right, is reduced by the traditional approach, Cage says, to a mere vehicle for the composer's ideas. In trying to detect his ideas, we, his "listeners," miss hearing the sound.

Cage wants modern music to divest itself of what he considers an encumbrance and liberate sound to be sound. For

Cage all sound—doorbells, car engines, hissing radiators—have an enchantment when we learn to hear them. However, the sound itself will only begin to come through to us, Cage says, if composers become the servants of sound. They must concentrate on providing a frame, a situation in which our attention is called to the sound, not as the medium for an idea but simply as a sound.

Cage's approach demolishes the very foundations of what we have thought of as music in the past. He carries through his program even in the way he arranges the sound situations. Since we have been prepared to listen for a developing pattern or theme that ties notes together in a configuration, again detracting our interest from the sound as such, he sometimes scores his music to be performed in sequences determined by the toss of a coin. He undermines the whole axiom of continuity by eliminating the idea of melody. We cannot listen to a note in terms of what has gone before. Thus both in his idea of what music is and in the way he puts sound together, Cage remains consistent. The present is radically severed from what has gone before.

Although Cage's ideas are widely discussed, he has certainly not exercised as much influence on modern music as Artaud has on theatre. It is true, of course, that today we admit a much wider range of sounds into what is accepted as "music." With the coming of electronic sound production, this process will continue to widen. Melody, however, lingers on and most people continue to prefer pianos and violins to radiators and truck engines. Still, Cage's ideas remain significant as symptoms of the incarnational prejudice against continuity. The past is immolated in the name of the present.

A Toast to Time

I have argued earlier in this chapter that late twentieth-century man finds himself in an "overheated history," that the death of

God goes together with man's bondage to history and detestation for it as two parts of a single process. In his panicky attempt to escape from history, man tries to destroy the past, in the interest either of the present or of the future. Both Cage and Artaud, for example, emphatically reject the past. They do so, however, for different reasons, and the difference is important. Artaud wants to draw people into an elemental confrontation that will shock and scar them but may evoke their own creative act. His theatre seeks to free us from the past so we can create something new. Cage, on the other hand, wants the composer and listener to stop creating and simply to hear what is there, to relish the audial feast we miss because conventional music has ruined us for it. Cage wants us to listen and be; Artaud wants us to feel and shape. For Cage the world is there to be accepted and enjoyed. For Artaud it is there to be encountered and recreated. What Artaud and Cage have in common with each other, and with an increasing proportion of our contemporary mentality is that they view the past not as friend but as foe, not as teacher but as oppressor. Continuity with what has gone before is not an achievement to be sought after but a bondage to be avoided.

Both these versions of today's contempt for the past have something to teach us, but both deteriorate very easily into perversions. The problem with Artaud is that he yearns so passionately for the new he often looks with hatred not only on what *was* but also on what *is*. His eschatology becomes fervid futurism. His compulsion to create the new curdles into a disgust for what is. It becomes what Nicola Chiaromonte, using a term from the history of religion, calls "gnosticism." Though gnosticism can mean many things, for Chiaromonte it means that Artaud hates the present material world. By "gnosticism," Chiaromonte says he means Artaud's "bottomless pessimism about the nature of the real world and his hatred of it, as a place of shadows and evil: which can be redeemed only by the effort of creation, the act of incarnating and personifying physically: for creation is a drive towards the light and the good. But it can never redeem completely. For in order to incarnate and personify, the creative act must accept matter, which is the principle of evil, and the form of the world as it is." [15]

Reality for Artaud is a spiritual struggle against a world that is not just inert but inherently destructive. The world, says Artaud, is a "phantom of humanity which is evil and malignant," bathed in the "lugubrious light of eroticism." Thus does Artaud reveal his disgust for the material, the sexual, even the body.

This is the danger of all longing for the future. It can easily collapse into not only a contempt for the past but a hatred for the present. The victims of this loathing are often the targets closest at hand, the earth, society, and even the human body. Both *earth* and *body* remind us every day of the past and of our undeniable continuity with it. Both bear the scars of former wounds and the marks of aging. If our abhorrence for the past becomes strong enough, we may turn to smashing the earth or to violating the body. Our present fascination with violence may be a symptom of our contempt for continuity. The tearing and burning of human flesh becomes a ritual by which we disentangle ourselves from cloying symbols of the past.

This gnostic hatred for the human body can be seen in our curious willingness as Americans to accept almost unlimited violence on the movie and television screens but to call the vice squad when an uncovered breast appears. Our censors snip the sex scenes out of Swedish movies while their censors cut the violent ones out of ours. Without even realizing it, most Americans have followed Artaud in rejecting the erotic and celebrating the violent. Hatred for the past when it springs from a compulsive desire for the new can result in a corrosive contempt for the present.

In the face of our culture's harried futurism, Cage's emphasis on what *is* comes as a refreshing corrective. It also, however, has its own dangers, dangers it shares, as we shall see, with the "now" emphasis of youth culture. Cage's invitation to us to frolic and gambol in what *is* can produce as its extreme a lack of any interest in hoping, creating, or changing. To express it again in the language of theology, a needed emphasis on *incarnation,* the presence of the spirit in the flesh can, if overdone, lead to a kind of presentism, a total absorption of interest in the here and now. This presentism can in turn slip over into a supine acceptance of the world as it is, and the consequent disappearance of fantasy, hope, revolt, or vision. It assumes a creation that is not only good but perfect. It looks forward to nothing and risks satiation and boredom. Since satisfaction with how things are now can easily lead to fear of change, it often becomes socially conservative.

Obviously, Artaud and Cage are merely symbols for two wider movements in our culture. Artaud illustrates the insistently anti-ideological and visionary quality of some of the student radicals. Although they do not share his contempt for the body, they do agree with him in his disdain for the present as well as for the past. Both Artaud and the young radicals oppose continuity in the interest of a future that is imagined mainly in its opposition to the present. Both love incantatory language. Both live on an abiding suspicion of almost everything that has ever happened before. Yet both are certainly correct in seeking to liberate us for a more fulfilling if still indistinct future.

Cage, on the other hand, symbolizes the mystical, Dionysiac, experience-oriented portion of the younger generation: the "now" mentality that is dedicated to the pursuit of direct experience, whether erotic, visual, or auditory. At its best it is immensely exciting. At its edges, however, like Cage's coin-tossing scores, it fades into the purposely slipshod technique of some underground cinema and into harmless or dangerous experimentation with drugs. In its sensate euphoria it can often overlook the gross injustices of the present and the need for a disciplined quest for social change.

Our culture in its spirited attempt to deliver us from our captivity to the past has collided with a theological problem, albeit one that few theologians recognize: how can we toast *all* the daughters of time? How can we celebrate the past, delight in the present, and gladly anticipate the future without sacrificing one to the other? The question must be asked: Does Christianity have anything to contribute to the solution of this problem?

Christianity asserts the goodness of the world but also recognizes that the world is vexed with imperfection, cruelty, and contradiction. It is good but fallen. Christianity teaches the presence of the divine in human flesh and, therefore, cannot accept the derogation or destruction of the flesh. It also contains an essentially future orientation. It looks forward to a New Era, an epoch of peace and human fulfillment. In such a vision man creates the new not because the world is evil but because its vivacity stimulates him to dance, sing, and symbolize. He hopes in the future because under the grim surface of things he can discern promise and possibility. Christianity fetes past, present, and future because without any one of them man would be the poorer.

As a consequence one might think that Christianity, because it does maintain such a fertile "mix" of time dimensions, would be able to assist contemporary society to put aside its fatal contempt for everything past. But it does not. Why? The reason is that in Christianity itself today the mix is badly distorted, with a bias not toward the present or the future but toward the past. To many observers, Christianity today personifies contempt for the flesh, a suspicion of sexuality, a distrust of present experience. Furthermore, Christianity seems to harbor a deep fear of the future and to live on a compulsive attachment to bygone ages. So long as this condition persists, no Christian corrective to our culture's contempt for the past will be possible.

The modern sensibility is correct in warning us that the past should have no favored status. It was not better, more virtuous, or closer to God. But in its crusade against the past, the modern sensibility has fallen into the snares of uncritical presentism and futurism, snares an alert theology might have helped it avoid. But theology is in no position to remove the mote from our culture's eye until it removes the beam from its own.

God and Festivity

Christianity was born and preached first in cultures in which feasts and celebrations were an organic and essential part of the whole world-view and way of life . . . And, whether we like it or not, Christianity accepted *and made its own this fundamentally human phenomenon of feast, as it accepted and made its own the whole man and all his needs.*

—*Alexander Schmemann,* Sacraments and Orthodoxy

The death of God is an experience of man. It has occurred in the life of modern industrial man because he has lost his capacity to live at once in history and in eternity, and to affirm all the dimensions of time as his friends. Preoccupied with producing and managing, he has lost touch with vast reaches of reality. His being has been harrowed and depleted. Therefore festivity is not just a luxury in life. It provides the occasion for man to reestablish his proper relation to time, history, and eternity. This is why only a rebirth of festivity can move us beyond the religious crisis we call the death of God.

We can understand how festivity liberates us from the death-of-God crisis only if we look carefully at the causes of the crisis itself. They are not to be found in Western religion alone but in a chain of events in which religion played only one, though a crucial, role.

It was indeed prophetic religion that directed the attention of Western man to history and its significance. It did so, however, not by divinizing history but by placing history in its larger setting and insisting on a fundamental link between these two spheres. The Israelites experienced the Holy One as crucially involved in history, but realized that history did not exhaust the reality of his being. However this was symbolized— Creation, Judgment, and so on—history became one dimension of a more inclusive reality. History was significant not just in itself but in its relation to something that exceeded it, of which it was an integral element. Man was able to see and appreciate history when, like a well-framed painting, it was placed in a setting that made it visible.

Marshall McLuhan and the Gestalt psychologists have both pointed out how this "framing" phenomenon operates. We cannot really "see" something if it fills in our whole visual environment. We need an "anti-environment" against which to make out its profile. The background or the field is an essential element in perception. Music on a concert stage we listen to. Music pumped into every closet and corridor by Muzak we may vaguely hear, but do *not* really listen to. Conversely an old automobile attracts our attention and becomes a work of "art" when it is removed from the highways and set on a display pedestal at a fair.

Without a larger frame history turns into something else. It becomes our total environment, and we begin to feel constricted and panicky. Thus the loss of a transcendent milieu radically alters our perception of history. Nietzsche saw this very clearly. After his madman announces the death of God in *The Gay Science,* he adds, "Must not we ourselves become Gods simply to seem worthy of it? There has never been a greater deed— for the sake of this deed he will be part of a higher history than all history hitherto." [16] What Nietzsche saluted as a "higher history" could just as easily be the "overheated history" that worries Lévi-Strauss or the overcommitment to history that concerns Richard Rubenstein. But despite what these thinkers sometimes advocate, twentieth-century man cannot now return to an archaic chrysalis, to earth goddesses and harvest festivals. He has now become irrevocably conscious of his historical being. He must learn to live in Nietzsche's "higher history." This fact has been expressed with unusual eloquence by Benjamin Nelson and Charles Trinkhaus in their introduction to a modern edition of Jacob Burckhardt's famous book on the Renaissance, that fateful period when this consciousness set its ineradicable seal on Western man.

Western man has irrevocably been cast out—has cast himself out—of a childlike world of enchantment and undividedness. Since the days of his exile (or was it withdrawal?) he has been wandering the world. Wherever he goes he is readily recognized since he bears a burden for everyone to see—the burden of selfhood. The ego is at once his sign of Cain and his crown of glory.[17]

Western man cannot and should not escape either his fragile but fantastic ego or its basis in his sense of historical consciousness. He should avoid the subtle allurement of futurism or presentism. What he needs, rather, is some way of restoring his vision of the wider reaches of his being and the relation between those wider reaches of reality and the historical part.

How can this vision be restored? This is a dilemma with which some of the most gifted thinkers of our age have grappled, albeit in different terms. In his *Meeting of East and West,* F. S. C. Northrop calls it the need to reconcile the "theoretic component" that he identifies with the West, and the "aesthetic component" that he sees exemplified by the East. Herbert Read tries to restore our sense of the primary role of the "iconic" in relation to "ideas" in the development of human consciousness.[18] Michael Polanyi calls our attention again to the "tacit dimension." [19] Others discuss the same problem in terms of the nonrational, sensuous, bodily components in perception and awareness.

But what does festivity have to do with all of this? Festivity is the way we cool history without fleeing from it. Festivity as both "legitimated excess" and as joy and juxtaposition plays an indispensable role in restoring to man his sense of the larger landscape within which history proceeds. It gives him a perspective on history without removing him from the terror and responsibility he bears as a history-maker. How? Let us look one more time at the phenomenon of festivity for our answer.

Many of our human celebrations are spur-of-the-moment affairs, like the sudden picnic or the party that erupts when friends drop in unexpectedly. But our most significant celebrations occur on stated occasions like Brazil's Carnaval or the all-night flings of high school seniors on commencement night. But in both spontaneous and scheduled celebrations we celebrate *something,* and that is a very important point. Festivity is never an end in itself. It expresses our joy *about* something. It celebrates something that has a place in human history, past or future.

But celebration is more than a mere affirmation of history. It also provides the occasion for a brief recess from history-making, a time when we are not working, planning, or recording. Hence the wise custom that outlaws talking business at parties. People who exploit festivals for purposes other than festivity endanger the festive air. Celebration, in short, reminds us that there is a side of our existence that is not absorbed in history-making, and therefore that history is not the exclusive or final horizon of life. As both an affirmation of history-making and a temporary respite from it, festivity reminds us of the link between two levels of our being—the instrumental, calculating side, and the expressive, playful side. Festivity periodically restores us to our proper relationship to history and history-making. It reminds us that we are fully within history but that history also is within something else.

In festivity, paradoxically, we both heighten our awareness of history and at the same time we take a brief vacation from history-making. The event we celebrate is historical, past or future, so it helps us to remember and hope. But during the celebration we stop *doing* and simply *are;* we move, as Norman Brown would say, from "becoming" to "being," and this also is crucial. If we had no past or future to celebrate, we would be trapped in an atemporal historyless present. On the other hand, if we were always busy making history but never celebrated it, we would be just as trapped in an unremitting treadmill from which all detachment, joy, and freedom were gone.

The disappearance of the divine milieu first makes history the sole reality for man and then forces him to escape its claustrophobic constriction by fleeing it. Festivity remains one of the few human actions where we keep our two environments in proper tandem. For this reason, festivity deserves more attention and more nourishment than it has been given by theologians or anyone else in the past. The "death of God" is a source as well as a symptom of our obsessive fixation on history today, and of our consequent hatred, fear, and attempt to escape it. The saddest sign of our sickness is that we have nearly forgotten how to live festively. But the most promising sign of hope is that here and there we are learning how again.

Perhaps when we have learned again to celebrate we will look back on the experience of God's death as merely the religious symptom of a cultural sickness—our worship of work and production, and our insensitivity to the mystery from which human history arises and toward which it inevitably flows.

A Dance Before the Lord 3

Do not cease dancing, you lovely girls! No killjoy has come to you with evil eyes, no enemy of girls. God's advocate am I before the devil: but the devil is the spirit of gravity. How could I, you lightfooted ones, be an enemy of Godlike dances? Or of girls' feet with pretty ankles?

—*Friedrich Nietzsche,* Thus Spoke Zarathustra

Postindustrial man is rediscovering festivity. The renaissance is a comprehensive one, not simply religious. But it goes a long way to explain the real significance of the recent eruption in the churches of multimedia masses, jazz rituals, folk and rock worship services, and dance liturgies. They are significant not in themselves but as indices of our culture's evaluation of certain modes of festivity. A people who dance before their gods are generally freer and less repressed than a people who cannot. This means that the argument about religion and the dance provides an interesting barometer to a much more fundamental cultural mood. How is that discussion now proceeding?

Some people reject the festive new liturgies as merely the latest example of ecclesiastical imperialism: religion exploiting flashy gimmicks to lure the recalcitrant back into the fold. Their apprehensiveness is well grounded. The church has often misused the arts in the past. Others argue that a good many of the innovations are of slapdash quality and that bad art has no rights of sanctuary, that it should be pursued and exposed wherever it shows up. They are right, too. Other people, however, oppose the guitar and the leotard in church for the same bad reasons their forebears opposed the use of the pipe organ— it had just never been done before, or so they think.

It is relatively easy to refute those who argue against trap drums behind the altar or religious dance simply on the grounds that there are no precedents. Take popular music, for example: although the church has a propensity to cling to the musical modes of the previous century, contemporary music, including popular tunes, has always managed to find its way back into worship. There has always been a John Wesley to ask why the devil should have all the good songs. Jazz, in one form at least, was born in the black church, and was first played in connection with funeral services. Wagons careened back from the cemetery playing "Didn't He Ramble." Though its short history has led jazz through many settings that are far from sanctimonious, its current contribution to the festive renewal of liturgy seems perfectly natural.

As for dance in the sanctuary, its history is a bit more complicated, but the precedents reach even further back. The Hebrew Scriptures are full of references to "dancing before the Lord," but it doesn't stop there. Dance held a real place in early Christian worship. The history of its rocky relations with Christianity—acceptance, excess, proscription, revival— is a fascinating one. Its highpoints are worth recalling because the story of religious dance is a parable of the spirit of festivity in Christianity.

In his scholarly history of religious dances, Professor E. Louis Backman documents the widespread use of dance not only in pre-Christian and pagan religious practices but in the Christian church itself.[1] It probably started very early. A document from the fourth century A.D. entitled *Quaestiones*, spuriously attributed to Justin Martyr who died in A.D. 165, recommends that children's choirs should not sing alone but should be accompanied by musical instruments, dancing, and rattles. Backman's research has persuaded him that for the early Christians these dancing choirs represented the angelic dance, and he points out that a boys' choir, dressed as angels, still dances before the altar in Seville. In the third century, Clement of Alexandria, who died in A.D. 216, had already de-

scribed in his "Address to the Heathens" a Christian initiation
ceremony in which torches, song and dancing in a ring "together with the angels" figure prominently.[2] Eusebius of Caesarea (died A.D. 339) tells of the way Christians danced before
God after the famous victory of Constantine: "With dances
and hymns in the cities and in the country they gave honor first
to the universal God . . . and then to the pious emperor." [3]
Christians danced a lot in the early years of the church. They
danced in places of worship and in churchyards. They danced
on saints' days and in cemeteries at the graves of martyrs. Men,
women, and children danced, before the Lord and with each
other.

Nevertheless, discomfort about dancing in church was developing quickly. The controversy appears openly in the fourth
century. St. Basil the Great, Bishop of Caesarea (A.D. 344–407)
is a key figure. He is important because he thoroughly approved
of church dance and in one of his sermons even extolled the
Christian life as a dance. Nevertheless, he was shocked at the
sensuality that he saw in the Easter dances and finally criticized
the women dancers in these very strong terms that could have
been written by a conservative bishop or staid elder last week:

*Casting aside the yoke of service under Christ . . . they . . .
shamelessly attract the attention of every man. With unkempt
hair, clothed in bodices and hopping about, they dance with
lustful eyes and loud laughter; as if seized by a kind of frenzy
they excite the lust of the youths. They execute ring-dances
in the churches of the Martyrs and at their graves, instead of
in the public buildings, transforming the Holy places into the
scene of their lewdness. With harlots' songs they pollute the
air and sully the degraded earth with their feet in shameful
postures.*[4]

St. Basil was against the dance for one reason—it was too
sensuous. Displaying that suspicion of flesh which has plagued

Christianity off and on for most of its history, he here clearly objects not to the dance as such, but to its explicitly sexual dimension.

For the next thousand years, the authorities of the church fought a hopeless battle, first to guarantee chasteness in the dance and, then, losing that struggle, to abolish it altogether. Century after century, bishops and councils issued decrees warning against various forms of dance in churches and church-yards. But they persisted. Finally, the Council of Würzburg in 1298 declared them a grievous sin.

Even this final interdiction, however, did not abolish religious dance. Proscribed from the sanctuary, the dancers moved to the square, the churchyard, and back to the cemetery. They tagged along at the edges of the processions, or sometimes took them over completely. They showed up on pilgrimages. They supplied the gusto at saints' days and festivals. Also in Christian movements outside the power of conciliar dicta dance worship continued, and persists to the present. In black congregations and Pentecostal churches, rhythmic movement has never disappeared. "Go forth, old men, young men and maidens," runs the exhortation of a Shaker elder a hundred years ago, "and worship God with all your might in the dance." [5]

A contemporary description of a Pentecostal service in Santiago, Chile, reminds us of how central dance, rhythm, and emotional expression have remained for millions of Christians who are sometimes mistakenly seen as "outside the mainstream of Christianity."

Meanwhile about 4,000 people had crowded into the church. In one gallery were a 200-voice choir and an orchestra with over 100 guitars, violins and mandolins. The singing began, in stepped-up rhythm, and soon the whole church was pulsing with vitality. As the singing progressed religious dancing appeared. Here and there, in the crowded pews and in the aisles, people began to move rhythmically with the music; some stomped on the floor, others moved round and round—gracefully, their arms moving to the beat of the music. On all faces were intense, rapt expressions; obviously, the people were lost in religious emotion.[6]

One need not fly to Chile to witness such effulgent festivity however. It rocks the roofs of black churches in every American ghetto and enlivens the spirit of poor whites in Holiness churches from Appalachia to Akron. The basic problem, of course, is that you cannot have dance without some element of sensuality. Dance both uses the body to celebrate and also celebrates the body. But most Christian theologians have harbored a persistent distrust of the body. Why? It may well result from the church's early brush with gnosticism, an ancient dualistic movement that was suspicious of the body. Some gnostics doubted that God could ever have created human flesh. Others allowed that God had created men, but surely not women, and one gnostic was of the opinion that God had created man only from the waist up. Christianity finally escaped from gnosticism but not without suffering a few scars. Thus Christianity has often tried to affirm the goodness of creation without delighting in human flesh. But this is simply not possible. The discomfort St. Basil felt at the "shameful postures" of the Easter dancers inevitably culminated centuries later in the Würzburg ban. His semignostic logic could have no other outcome.

This means we should be fully appreciative of the deeper significance of the return of rhythmic movement to the church. It means the festival spirit, heretofore relegated to the annex, has returned to the sanctuary. It is a mistake to try to defend jazz and modern dance by pretending that they are not sensuous and that therefore it is perfectly safe to allow them in church. They *are* sensuous and they are *not* "safe." As E. R. Dodds, one of the great scholars of the origins of religious dance, says: "The Power of the Dance is a dangerous power. Like other forms of self-surrender, it is easier to begin than to stop." [7] At points, many dances are explicitly erotic, but this is just what is important about them. They represent a postgnostic, perhaps more accurately a post-Victorian form of Christianity. As the Roman Catholic writer Paul Valery says:

The Dance, in my opinion, is much more than an exercise, an entertainment, an ornament, a society pastime; it is a serious thing and, in some respects, even a holy thing. Every age which has understood the human body, or which has, at least, sensed something of the mystery of this structure, of its resources, of its limitations, of the combinations of energy and sensibility which it contains, has cultivated, venerated the Dance.[8]

In our own age a festive faith is now ready to celebrate in the flesh and to rejoice in the fact that neither the sensuousness of the dance nor the earthiness of jazz makes it an unfit vehicle for the praise of God. Describing this rebirth of festivity in what has sometimes been called the "underground church," Roman Catholic lay theologian Michael Novak declares that it "offers a way of celebrating death and life, community and loneliness, joy and sadness—a way that is at once fresh and spontaneous and yet tied to tradition as old as Western man." He adds that although the movement is taking place mainly among middle-class people, it is turning middle-class society "in the direction of spontaneity, touch, dance, emotion, and noise—i.e., in a direction historically more congenital to primitive societies and the poor." [9] Another lay theologian, William Birmingham, calls this whole phenomenon "the eroticization of liturgy." [10] In what may be excessively male-oriented terms he says, "I like to imagine a liturgy that is as attractive as a beautiful woman." We should first *experience* liturgy, Birmingham says, and then think about it later. Not vice versa.

All this does not mean we must welcome every awkward

rhythm choir or every "rock mass" with open arms. Much of what happens under these titles in churches today is either tasteless and boring, or a blatant attempt to con people back into expiring churches. But neither should we underestimate the long-range significance of the new openness of Christianity to forms of expression from which it has sometimes recoiled in the past. Festivals, once pushed to the edge of religious life, have come back into its center. Christians are learning not to shudder at festal excess but to welcome it. The Cageian quest for immediate access to the banquet of existence appears here in the nasal twang of an electric guitar and the symmetry of bodies in motion. The style makes all the difference. The medium becomes part of the message. People who have rejected Christian ideas in their didactic form can sometimes affirm them in festivity. Some who cannot say a prayer may still be able to dance it.[11] People who cannot hope may be able to laugh.

There are those who argue that this playful air represents a perversion of the faith. I think they are wrong. For such people the gravity of conventional Christianity is its normal and even normative style. The truth may very well be that we have inherited a recently perverted form of Christianity, that its terrible sobriety is a distortion of its real genius, and that a kind of playfulness lies much closer to its heart than solemnity does. The devil, Nietzsche claims, is "the spirit of gravity." And a Christian mystic in the tradition of St. Bernard once wrote these lines:

Jesus the dancers' master is,
A great skill at the dance is his,
He turns to right, he turns to left;
All must follow his teaching deft.[12]

The appearance in our time of Christ the harlequin and the Lord of the Dance should provide a double cause for rejoicing.

Not only does he draw us in to the dance of life, he also restores an essential aspect of our faith that in the awful seriousness of our age we had nearly forgotten.

In any case, regardless of its eventual theological consequences, the fact of resurgent festivity is undeniable. Something of the jubilant, even the Dionysiac, is returning in force to contemporary Christianity. Joyous movement, radiant color, and piercing sound are no longer interdicted. Man affirms the flesh in the house of God. What is even more important however is the rebirth of festivity in the culture at large. What Christianity permits to happen in church buildings is important mainly as a clue to what it encourages in the culture. An anti-festive church drives the dancers not only out of the temple but out of the streets and houses, too, if it has the power. Likewise, a church that encourages the affirmation of the body within the sacred precinct itself may lend its support to a less repressive social order.

What eventually happens to the church or to liturgical dancing is not a matter of urgent concern in itself. What happens to our stifled, sensually numbed culture is important. To reclaim the body, with all its earthy exquisiteness in worship is a hopeful sign only if it means we are ready to put away our deodorants and prickliness and welcome the body's smell and feel back into our ascetic cultural consciousness. Only when that happens will we know that our civilization has left behind the gnostics and their wan successors and has moved to a period when once again we can talk about the redemption of the body without embarrassment.

Part Two

Fantasy: The Ingredients 4

O fantasy, that at times does so snatch us out of
Ourselves that we are conscious of naught, even
Though a thousand trumpets sound about us,
Who makes thee, if the senses set naught before thee?
A light moves thee which takes its form in heaven, of
Itself, or by a will that sendeth it down.

—*Dante,* The Divine Comedy

Fantasy like festivity reveals man's capacity to go beyond the empirical world of the here and now. But fantasy exceeds festivity. In it man not only relives and anticipates, he remakes the past and creates wholly new futures. Fantasy is a humus. Out of it man's ability to invent and innovate grows. Fantasy is the richest source of human creativity. Theologically speaking, it is the image of the creator God in man. Like God, man in fantasy creates whole worlds *ex nihilo,* out of nothing.

Yet, despite its importance, our era has dealt very shabbily with fantasy. In many other cultures fantasy has been carefully nurtured and those with unusual abilities at fantasy honored. In ours, we have ignored fantasy, deprecated it, or tried to pretend it wasn't really there. After all, *we* are "realists."

Why do we take such a dim view of fantasy? One reason is that as a hard-nosed, pragmatic, problem-solving culture, we do not want to be distracted by something so evanescent. We divide the world into two spheres: the world of fact and the world of fantasy. As the true heirs of our Puritan forebears, we are taught to turn our backs on the world of fantasy—along with such accompaniments as mirth, intemperance, and unseemly speculation—to labor diligently in the world of facts. That very Puritan man, Sigmund Freud, sternly warned us to respect the "reality principle" and not to be tricked by "illusion," future or otherwise.

So we have obeyed. We have drawn a line between fact and fantasy, and allowed the term "reality" to be used only for the former. Yet, "reality" is hardly a clear and distinct idea.[1] What is "reality" for one society is illusion for another. "Reality" is not a fixed or changeless category. It is what a particular culture decides it will be. Thus, in some oriental cultures, much of what we call the "factual world" is viewed as unreal, at the same time some societies find reality in the dreams, visions, and fantasies that we mark down as illusory. There is no final arbiter about what is "really real." Science is not designed to demonstrate what is real, but to investigate that portion of reality for which its methods are appropriate.

Our present Western definition of reality is unfortunately a narrow one. Nor is our Puritan heritage the only cause for our nearsightedness. So is our awe of tools and materials. As Lewis Mumford has shown we have become so fascinated with early man as the tool-maker we have forgotten that before he made tools, he made myths and rituals.[2] In addition, our moralistic religious history in America has taught us to be suspicious of any activity that appears to waste time or does not seem to serve the concrete interests of the commonwealth. In the introduction to one of his novels, Nathaniel Hawthorne speculates that his stern, gray New England forebears would have been just as distressed at his becoming a writer as they would have been at his becoming a fiddler. The comparison is instructive. The Puritan mentality was suspicious both of spinning tales and of musical merry-making. Church, factory, office, laboratory, and classroom have all conspired to assign fantasy a back seat.

All of this has been true up until very recently. Today, however, there are indications that we may be ready not only to reinstate fantasy, but perhaps even to begin redefining reality so that fantasy is not left completely out. "The ability to 'fantasize,' " says the science-fiction master Ray Bradbury, "is the ability to survive." [3] He is not alone in his opinion. Even the most fact-obsessed technician today recognizes that those who make the research breakthroughs are more often the dipsy-dreamers than the relentless grinds. Many companies have even instituted "brainstorming" sessions to stimulate imagina-tion. Historians of science now assign more importance than they once did to hunches, insights, and creative flashes. They insist that real advances in science come when someone leaps out of existing paradigms and creates a new way of envisioning things.[4] In politics, utopian fancy is no longer ruled out as wholly irrelevant. Albert Camus sees the unfettered imagina-tion as one way we "contest reality" and create history. It is part of what he calls the "metaphysical rebellion."

We have all begun to recognize that change is vital to our lives and that a changing society needs its share of dreamers and visionaries. Once again we have begun to ask such ques-tions as: What is the source of the new? Where do change and innovation come from? How can creativity be nourished and stimulated? Such questions have led us to take a closer look at what we had formerly dismissed as "mere" imagination, day-dreaming, or fantasy. An alert schoolteacher today will not conclude that the boy with the dreamy expression in the fourth row is merely "wool-gathering" and should be called to atten-tion. He may be off on a "fantasy trip" that should not be interrupted.

In short, fantasy is no longer a subject only for the student of the trivial. We are now ready to ask what we mean by fantasy, to mention some of the recent scientific work that has been done on the subject, and then to take a fresh look at it from a theological perspective.

Most writers use the words "imagination" and fantasy inter-changeably. I would like to make a distinction. In imagination, we set aside for a moment our usual decorum and social inhibi-tion. This imagination in all its forms resembles the "legitimated excess" of celebration. This is why the costume party, in which we playfully suspend for awhile our normal roles and become pirates and princesses will always have a place. At the Halloween party and the masked ball, imagination and celebration merge.[5] As in the Feast of Fools, we see their natural consanguinity.

Imagination opens doors that are normally closed to us. Through its power we sneak into forbidden situations, we explore terrifying territory, we try out new styles. We may tell off a boss, seduce a gorgeous woman, or even run a spear through an annoying neighbor. Or we sketch the outline of a situation we will soon face, and rehearse our performance. We can even see ourselves a year ago or a year hence, and speculate on what might have been or what may be. All these are familiar functions of the imagination.

Fantasy, as I shall use the word, is "advanced imagining." In fantasy, no holds are barred. We suspend not only the rules of social conduct, but the whole structure of everyday "reality." In fantasy we become not only our ideal selves, but totally different people. We abolish the limits of our powers and our perception. We soar. We give reign not only to socially discouraged impulses but to physically impossible exploits and even to logically contradictory events. Fantasy is the habitat of dragons, magic wands, and instant mutations. It is the waking state that borders most closely on the realm of sleeping dreams. But unlike dreams, in fantasy there is an element of art and conscious creativity.

There are perils when fantasy loses its link to reason and fact. Some of the people we call mentally ill are simply more at home in the precinct of fantasy. There are other people, however, and we call them "sane," who tremble to approach its borders, afraid perhaps that they will never get back. They are the dull, predictable drudges of the world, living starved and shrunken lives. If they ever do have a vision they are terrified by it, scared that if they admitted it they might land with the so-called "mentally ill" inside asylum bars.[6]

Most of us are neither churls nor lunatics. We live on the border of factland and fantasia, and we commute back and forth, but we are secretly puzzled about how the two fit together, if at all. Also, few of us have given much thought to the fantasy world as a source of renewal in the fact world. Freud, for example, devoted a considerable portion of his career to the analysis of nightdreams, but he paid little attention to daydreams. Fantasy, since it is made of much the same stuff that dreams are made of, is a difficult subject to study. Until quite recently most of the writing about it had a somewhat cabalistic flavor. But all that is now changing. We have become less nervous about fantasy and some formerly cautious people are even suggesting that it plays a positive role in life. For example, the British scholar J. R. R. Tolkien, who has combined in one career both scholarly writing and the creation of fantasy, says,

Fantasy is a natural human activity. It certainly does not destroy or even insult Reason; and it does not either blunt the appetite for, nor obscure the perception of, scientific verity. On the contrary. The keener and the clearer is the reason, the better fantasy it will make. If men were ever in a state in which they did not want to know or could not perceive truth (facts or evidence) then Fantasy would languish until they were cured.[7]

An example of recent research is provided by the work of Jerome L. Singer and John Antrobus, who have worked both on fantasy and daydreaming. They have discovered a number of interesting points and confirmed some hunches most of us had already. Daydreams, they report, after extensive questionnaire research, "take the form of fairly clear visual images" and "occur chiefly during private moments, just before bedtime or during rides on trains or buses." [8] This much is hardly news.

More intriguingly, however, they also found that individuals who were very close to their mothers or who had rejected their father's values daydreamed more frequently and more creatively. They also found that Anglo-Saxons daydream less than Jews and Italians, and that black people daydream more frequently than any other group. Unfortunately, the subjects of their investigations were mostly college-educated people, so comparisons among socioeconomic classes were not possible.

Still, the conclusions to which Singer and Antrobus come, even though tentative, offer some fascinating food for thought. For example, if it is true that black people in America seem to have a richer and more extensive fantasy life than other people do, this could mean there is a positive correlation between fantasy and what sociologists have sometimes called "marginality." Maybe groups and individuals who are cut out of the benefits of a given society are the ones who most often dream about another, and sometimes act to bring it about.

Man's openness to a really new future is dependent on his capacity for fantasy. Fantasy thrives among the dissatisfied. This suggests that insight into the future and willingness to move forward may require an element of alienation from our present society. Could this be why Jesus insisted that only the poor and the disinherited could really grasp the Kingdom of God?

Also, let us accept for the moment that closeness to one's mother or the rejection of one's father's values correlates with high fantasy. If we add to this our knowledge that fantasy and festivity somehow support each other, we can ask whether this sheds any light on the sources of fantasy and festivity in countries with maternal rather than paternal religious symbolism? In Mexican folk Catholicism, for example, Our Lady of Guadaloupe is immeasurably more central than either God or Christ. In middle-class Protestant America, God is a hard-working Presbyterian father. In most societies, the father stands for the no-nonsense world of problems to be solved and work to be done. The mother, more often, is the one who encourages or at least tolerates fantasy. We know that the Mexican capacity for festivity exceeds anything in largely Protestant North America. It would be interesting to know about comparative levels of fantasy.

Singer and Antrobus did not indulge in such cultural and theological speculation. They did decide, however, that daydreaming cannot be explained by the early psychoanalytic theory which held that fantasy merely compensates us by providing in fancy the things we would like but cannot get in reality. Nor is fantasy just a defense mechanism or a safe way of channeling natural drives. Though daydreaming may serve such functions, these investigators believe it is a much more complex thing. It springs from the brain's ongoing activity and is an ability, like perception or cognition, that can either be developed and expanded, or discouraged and stunted.

Perhaps the most interesting recent work on fantasy, however, comes from France. There, two psychologists, Roger Frétigny and André Virel, both of whom also have interests in philosophy, art, and anthropology, began sometime ago to use what they called "directed fantasy" in therapy. This method, sometimes called the "guided daydream," was not new, but in their work, Frétigny and Virel brought together a number of previously disparate techniques and discovered a world of fascinating things about "mental imagery." In a recent book, they have presented their findings and skillfully related them to previous work on mental imagery in anthropology and comparative religion.[9] I believe that this work has immeasurable importance for theology.

For Frétigny and Virel, the imagination, of which fantasy is the essential expression, is not simply one faculty among others, but occupies a "central and determinative role in the history of the psyche." They refuse to rank fantasy lower than other forms of mental activity or to concede that in fantasy we are less "conscious" than we are in other states. They list four types of consciousness—imaginative, active, reflexive, and contemplative —each one of which has a significant function of its own. Among these, the imaginative, of which fantasy is the prime example, not only systematizes the materials of experience but takes apart both materials and systems in order to construct new configurations. Why do we need imagination? We need it because the substance of the universe of thought is just too changing and too complex to be appropriated in a merely rational manner. Therefore, it is the job of the imagination "to operate a dialectic of the real and the possible." Without it, "discursive thought would become incurably crippled in a closed and ossified system." [10]

Those who study fantasy today agree that it has various forms—reverie, imaginative action, creation—and that they all play a decisive role in life. Both persons and groups establish rhythms of movement back and forth between the world of facts and the world of fantasies. For individuals, the rhythm is relatively fast. We may fantasize after only minutes of attention to the fact world. In groups the rhythm is slower. In tribal societies, the period of group fantasy corresponds to the seasonal celebrations of the myths and legends of the tribe. In more complex societies, it is not as well-marked and may come less frequently. Virel and Frétigny even speculate that civilizations go through long alternating periods. For centuries they will devote obsessive attention to the fact world, but this will then be followed by a period of imaginative creativity and heightened fantasy. Afterwards there is another fact era and so on.

This may suggest why our own period is one in which we both suspect fantasy but are becoming more fascinated with it. We have spent the last few hundred years with our cultural attention focused fixedly on the "outside" factual world— exploring, investigating, and mastering it. Those with a penchant for fantasy never really felt at home. But now there are signs that a new age of fantasy is about to begin, that there are new worlds to explore. We may be on the threshold of an

exciting period of symbol formation and myth creation. It
could be an age in which the fantasy side of our civilization
once again flowers. During the coming period, which Nicholas
Berdyaev thought would be a "new middle ages," we may take
apart the elements of our existing perceptual apparatus and re-
construct it on wholly new lines.

Frétigny and Virel, however, do not go this far. They do refer
favorably, though, to a tribe in New Guinea which daydreams
its cosmology and then illustrates it in beautifully worked
masks. Then each year the masks are burned so that the imagination can exercise its right to create living myths. As a culture
we may now be in the midst of a similar process. Many of our
myths and masks have already been burned, though so far few
new ones have emerged to take their place. In any case, these
observations on myths, masks, and imagination, as well as our
speculations on the rhythmic pattern of fantasy and cognition
bring us to the question of religion and its relation to fantasy.

Fantasy and Religion 5

Fantasy and Myth

Myth is the dream-thinking of a people, just as the dream is the myth of the individual.

—*Jane Harrison,* Epilogomena to the Study of Greek Religion

Myth is an essential part of religion, but religion is more than myth. Starting with the reinstatement of fantasy that we have just documented in the last chapter, however, we can now say that religion is to a civilization what fantasy is to an individual. Like fantasy, religion requires special occasions and a special type of consciousness, but has an important if not constitutive influence on all occasions and on all types of consciousness. Like fantasy, religion delights in symbols, in the transmutation of familiar forms, and in the elaboration of impulses and ideas beyond the confines of empirical limitations. Like fantasy, religion enables man to transcend the empirical world and to appreciate the sublimity and mystery of existence.

Ordinarily, to compare religion with fantasy might appear to downgrade or even to dismiss religion. It should be clear by now, however, that this is not my intention. If the research discussed in the previous chapter is right when it claims that fantasy plays a "central and determinative role" in the history of human development, then to compare religion with fantasy is not to derogate it but to insist on its importance.

Applying recent research on fantasy to religion yields even further insights. It permits us to see that in any given civilization, religion not only organizes and lends value to experience, it also occasionally breaks apart its patterns and reorganizes perception on a wholly new basis. When we build on the premise that reality goes beyond the fact world and includes the fantasy world, relating religion to fantasy in no way denies the reality of religion.

All great civilizations begin, as Arnold Toynbee has shown, with a religious impetus. They do not stay there, however, just as a person cannot remain a child. Any civilization that does not move beyond its original religious impulse is clinging to infancy. It will never reach critical maturity. But on the other hand, a civilization that loses touch entirely with the fantasy world, that fears and represses its religious sources, is just as badly off. It is like a person pursued by a past he is afraid to accept. The style of such a civilization becomes either "closed and ossified" or obsessively voguish. Either it is afraid to risk breaking its secular masks or it is incapable of allowing the imagination to create new ones. Without secularization a culture gropes forever in the lurid world of fantasy. But without fantasy a society cuts itself off from the visceral fonts of renewal. Like individuals, civilizations can neither crouch in their pasts nor repudiate them. They must learn to live with them creatively. Nor can they exist entirely either in the night world or in the day world. An alternation is needed and fantasy provides the bridge. It is a twilight or dawn phenomenon—the waking state that is closest to dreams. It is also a dream state in which nonetheless we remain fully awake. Like religion, it links past, present, and future, and spans the two worlds in which man is fated to live.

But merely comparing religion with fantasy is neither very new nor very helpful. Fantasy, like religion, can hurt as well as help. It can lure us into madness and destruction. It can provide a handy escape hatch through which we can scurry to avoid the problems of the world. This may be why primitive peoples, sensing the fearsome ambiguity of the holy, carved ferocious monsters on the mantles of their temples and spilled blood on their altars. We should also be aware of the demonic side of fantasy. Furthermore, the mere comparison of religion and fantasy does not take into account either the difference between historical and cosmic religions, or between myth and event. Nor does it uncover the significance of biblical faith for religion and fantasy. What then is the real relation between fantasy and religion?

In answering this question we run into certain difficulties. Just as Protestant theologians have written very little on the subject of festivity, perhaps as a result of the Protestant pre-occupation with the moral and intellectual aspects of religion, so also there is very little written either by Protestant or Catholic theologians on fantasy. In fact, there is not much theological literature on this subject at all. There is, however, a long tradition, especially in Roman Catholic thought, of at-tention to what has sometimes been called "intuition" or "theoria," a type of thinking that is not immediately concerned with solving problems but is more or less pure thought. "The-oria," according to this tradition, is to pragmatic thinking what play is to work. It is free, noninstrumental, and engaged in for its own sake. As Josef Pieper says, "theoria" occurs only when we see the world as something more than a field for human accomplishment.[1] "Theoria," like fantasy, is an activity that defies all existing canons of the "useful" or the "realistic." By putting together what Catholic thinkers have said about "the-oria" with what Protestants have said about "myth," we come close to a theology of fantasy.

Fantasy and Ritual

Ritual provides both the form and the occasion for the expres-sion of fantasy. It is through ritual movement, gesture, song, and dance that man keeps in touch with the sources of creativ-ity. Ritual appeared along with myth in man's development, and springs from the same sources. In ritual, men "act out" the reveries and hopes of the tribe. Ritual humanizes space as myth humanizes time.

Ritual is social fantasy. It is very similar to celebration and in some ways indistinguishable from it. But have we not outgrown ritual? Has it not, like magic potions and alchemy, fled before the march of science and secularization?

I do not think so. Although traditional religious rituals may be declining in some places, ritual itself, as symbolic movement and the patterned enactment of fantasy, has not. But ritual has fallen on evil days. It has moved in two directions, toward the *ideological* on the one hand and the *idiosyncratic* on the other. Both represent perversions of the essential human significance of ritual.

Ritual becomes *ideology* when it is used to throttle creativity, to channel religion or fantasy into safely accepted molds. Organized religions in periods of decline, nations anxious to enforce patriotism and obedience, individuals who feel they may be losing a grip on themselves—all become self-conscious and meticulous about ritual proprieties. Enforced ritual, handed down from above, chokes off spontaneity and petrifies the spirit. True, like the Nazi rituals, it may temporarily bring a sick kind of order to a deranged society, or it can produce a spurious appearance of unity in a church. But this order and unity are bought at a terrible price. Freedom, hope, and joy are sacrificed and what remains is the empty shell of calcified gesture. When ritual is used as a vehicle for promulgating an ideology, the ritual is prostituted and the ideology soon withers.

Yet, today, we are weighted down by numberless ideological rituals, both political and ecclesiastical. We stand up for national anthems and salute flags in a day when nation-states have become antiques. In church, we doze through rituals that lack any living meaning. Schools, colleges, businesses, and families use once-vital ritual forms to keep people in line or to foster some ideology. For some, grace at table is only a way to quiet the kids.

When Freud investigated ritual, he decided it was a type of obsessional neurosis. He saw people pathetically repeating the same action over and over, like Lady Macbeth washing her hands, because they were incapable of facing a world that would require something new. Freud was right as far as he went. But just as his investigation of fantasy centered mainly on its defensive and compensatory side, his understanding of ritual was also limited. What he saw were religious rituals in their distorted condition. Ideology is the social equivalent of neurosis and rituals are its symptoms, the spastic gestures anxious groups use to express their collective dementia. But all fantasy behavior on the part of individuals is not neurotic. Some of it is pioneering, the personal "embodiment" of untried insights. Likewise, not all ritual is ideological. Just because an action is patterned, or performed by more than one person, or has symbolic ingredients, does not make it repressive or neurotic. Ritual can be liberating. People burn tyrants' flags as well as salute them. They can shake their fists as well as bow their heads. Symbolic movement can be used to liberate man, not just to oppress him.

What then is a liberating ritual? Before we examine that question, let us look at the other contemporary perversion of ritual, the *idiosyncratic*.

Ritual becomes *idiosyncratic* when it ceases to be shared by a group or to emerge from historical experience, when it becomes the property of just one, or of just a few people. Men have always expressed their deepest joys, fears, and longings in acts, shouts, jumps, gestures, and struts. Such throes only later develop into a patterned ritual with a mythic meaning. Still, until a gesture achieves social significance, and is felt or appreciated by someone else, it remains something less than human. Ritual provides a set of connections through which emotion can be *ex*pressed without being *re*pressed. This is why we have called ritual "social fantasy."

But as rituals are laden first with myths and then with doctrines, they grow less flexible. Gestures stagger under the weight of the explicit meanings we load onto them. Emotions well up that cannot be expressed within them. When tribes with different rituals meet, things may go well if their rituals are not too explicitly defined. But if their meanings have been nailed down, communication at a deeper level becomes difficult. Think of the strife caused by all the efforts to explain communion as "trans-" or "con-" substantiation. As definitions pile up and ideology intrudes, people become frustrated by the rigidity and inadequacy of existing ritual systems; they begin to "roll their own." Sects, schisms, and underground churches appear. They have for centuries.

There is nothing wrong with inventing rituals. All rituals were at one time invented by someone. But if man wants to express his deepest feelings to himself and to other men, ritual must have a social dimension. And if man is to be in touch with what others have sensed in the dim past, or if he wants to pass on his experience to the future, the ritual must have a historical dimension as well. Furthermore, even to express his deepest feelings to himself, man needs a ritual, just as he needs a language even to talk to himself. Ritual does for movement what language does for sound, transforms it from the inchoate into the expressive. Therefore an idiosyncratic ritual is ultimately frustrating and self-defeating.

Ritual is "embodied fantasy." The word "body" is important. It indicates that in ritual fantasy is not merely mental. Gesture and movement are also important. The word "body" also signifies a historical and social location. Our body places us. It came from our parents and through it we touch, punch, caress, and pass life on to the future. Likewise in ritual, fantasy feeds back into history, touches other men, and reaches toward the future. It does not simply zoom in the ether. In fantasy, our physical body is left behind and an imaginary body, often differing markedly from the physical one, takes over. Thus, one of the things "fantasy therapy" does is to help the client integrate these two bodies. It does so, however, not by chopping the fantasy body down to size, but by letting the fantasy body infuse and transform the physical one. Fantasy "connects" and performs its function only when it is "embodied."

In the previous chapter we mentioned the research on fantasy carried on by André Virel and Roger Frétigny. Their discussion of the physical body and the fantasy body has important theological implications that they do not, of course, develop. It suggests a reason why Christianity has stubbornly stuck to what seems to be the incredible notion of the "resurrection of the body," rather than accepting the more "spiritual" idea of the "immortality of the soul." Ideas or fantasies that are not "embodied" have little reality for Christianity. The idea of the resurrection of the body suggests an interactive relation between the "fact" world and the "fantasy" world that gives each its due. Both worlds are "real" worlds. So both the hard-headed citizens who enclose themselves completely in facts and the flipped-out individuals who live only in fantasy inhabit truncated worlds, sealed off from full reality. Christianity sticks obstinately to the resurrection of the body. This ties it indissolubly to earth, flesh, and history. On the other hand, the fact that no one can "make sense" of the resurrection, that it does not fit nicely into the "fact world" is also important. It keeps us alert to that larger reality that is not fully exhausted by "facts".

If ideology and idiosyncrasy represent perversions of ritual, what is authentic ritual? Here an analogy from the field of linguistics may help. The comparative study of languages indicates that a language, in its vocabulary, grammar, and syntax, provides a formal structure for expression. Any language will have certain built-in assumptions in its structure, but no language really "says" anything as such. It provides the speaker who really commands that language with the opportunity of saying anything he chooses. Paradoxically then, we must speak within a language, even when we criticize its assumptions. A language, at one and the same time, *imposes* a structure on us and *allows* us to rebel against and criticize the structure. Even James Joyce, who grossly violated the rules of grammar and boldly invented new words, did so using the structure of the English language, of which he was a master. He had to assume that his readers would know English, if only to be able to notice his violations.

A liberating ritual is one that provides the formal structure within which freedom and fantasy can twist and tumble. It provides the person with a series of movements in which he is given access to an enormous wealth of human feelings. But these feelings now become the material for his own escapades in creativity. The best analogy to a liberating ritual may still be the jazz combo or dixieland band. The chord structure and rhythm conventions provide the base from which spectacular innovations and individual *ad libs* can spin out. Without such a structure, the music would deteriorate into cacophony. With it, the individual players not only climb to musical peaks, but often they stimulate each other to explore unexpected vistas of sound.

Ritual is that form of human action which both nourishes fantasy and embodies it in society and history. But one major question remains. Which of the great traditional rituals shall we choose as our environment for fantasy? Is one ritual as good as another? What is the particular significance of the rituals associated with Christianity?

Fantasy and Christianity

And it shall come to pass afterward, that I will pour out my spirit on all flesh; your sons and your daughters shall prophesy, your old men shall dream dreams, and your young men shall see visions. Even upon the menservants and maidservants in those days, I will pour out my spirit.

—*Joel 2:28–29 (RSV)*

In the biblical tradition visions and dreams are an important means God uses to communicate with man. But not all visions and dreams come from God. There are false prophets and seers as well as true ones. Still, even though the problem of distinguishing between the true and the false was a taxing one, the importance of visions, and their reality, was never denied. In the New Testament both St. Peter and St. Paul had visions. So did St. John, and the imagery of his ecstatic experiences makes the book of Revelation one of the most intriguing in the entire Bible. During the course of Christian history the reality of visions has been kept alive by two traditions, both of them sometimes viewed with suspicion by the official hierarchy.[2] The first is the tradition of mysticism and contemplation. The second is that of utopian and apocalyptic faith. In Chapter 6 I will discuss the utopian tradition. Here I want to deal with those aspects of the Christian liturgy that encourage and sustain fantasy and vision.

For psychotherapists who see the value of fantasy, the purpose of therapy is not simply to "adjust" clients to the world of facts. Nor, obviously, is it to make them feel entirely at home in the world of fantasy. Rather, it is to help the client construct the kind of experiential bridge between these two worlds that will both heighten the adventure of fantasy and lead to maximum creativity. The object of their therapy is the *creative* person, not the adjusted person. How do they proceed?

The methods are too varied and complex to recount in full, but one frequently used procedure is important for our purposes. It is a technique its originator, the French psychiatrist Robert Desoille calls the "rêve éveillé dirigé" (the directed waking dream), and it has been developed into a remarkable therapeutic method.[3] This approach has also been used by psychiatrists at the Esalen Institute and elsewhere. It calls for inducing in the client a relaxed but still wakeful state, and then suggesting to him certain basic themes on which he is invited to elaborate his own fantasies. The themes are the equivalent of the jazz chord structure; they invite invention and elaboration.

In their many years of treatment and experimentation, André Virel and Roger Frétigny have sorted out three types of themes.[4] The first they call "images carrefours" (nodal images). These are the images that have appeared most frequently in spontaneous fantasy. The second, "images clés" (key images), are the ones that most vividly reveal some aspect of the psyche or else vault the client to a new level of fantasy. The last, "images de securisation" (reassurance images), are introduced when a client comes to some obstacle in his fantasy or is inhibited by fear or anxiety. The reassurance image gives him the courage to proceed with his fantasy. It is important to emphasize that in all of this the client is encouraged not only to use these images in whatever way he wants, but to add his own and to combine them in any way he chooses.

Therapists who use directed fantasy have discovered in their practice that very few people feel limited by the skillful introduction of these various themes. For most people just the opposite occurs. The timely injection of such images not only enormously enhances their capacity for fantasy, it also greatly facilitates the creative combining of the physical self and the imaginary self.

The practice of guided fantasy is not new to religion. It is strikingly similar in many ways to the method of meditation outlined in the sixteenth century by Ignatius Loyola in his *Spiritual Exercises*.[5] In one famous section, for instance, St. Ignatius advocates what he calls the "application of the senses," using imaginary taste, touch, smell, and sight to experience the torments of hell or the transports of heaven. The same kind of guided fantasy may be taking place in such standard Catholic devotions as the recitation of the rosary and praying at the stations of the cross.

Both in traditional forms of piety and in "guided fantasy" therapy, we have examples of how structure can facilitate freedom. Even in the fantasy world, man is a social-historical animal, and he is freed to create on his own by the proper use of themes and images drawn from the wider experience of the race.

But if we look carefully at the themes used in the "directed waking dream," we also notice something else. These themes bear a striking resemblance to those that appear in Christian ritual. "Nodal images" suggest the universal elements of aspiration, awe, gratitude, and joy that Christian ritual shares not only with all religions but with most of ordinary experience. "Key images" recall the notion of crisis and challenge that is associated with the call to decision and the necessity of making a responsible choice. The "reassurance images" suggest those rituals in which God's forgiveness is announced and celebrated, the new way is opened, the renewed life is made possible. In other words, the dynamics of the images used in such therapy strikingly resemble the central dimensions of Christian liturgy.

They are not, of course, totally dissimilar from other traditional religious rituals. Nor do fantasy therapists utilize exclusively the imagery of any particular religious tradition. However, two points should be mentioned about this method of therapy. Both provide interesting analogies with Christianity in particular.

First, the object of fantasy therapy is to effect a viable connection between the two aspects of reality we have called fact and fantasy. It does so by taking the fact world very seriously, but not ultimately. Fantasy therapy never derogates the gritty reality of the historical-social world of bothersome relatives, noisy streets, and encrusted institutions. It operates on the assumption, now widely accepted but biblical in origin, that the factual world is *not* illusory but a crucial part of the total reality with which we have to do. This is not an assumption that would comport well with some aspects of Eastern religious thought in which the everyday world is somehow seen as unreal or illusory. Fantasy therapists operate, even if they are not wholly conscious of it, on the biblical assumption of a creation and a history which are *there* and which we must deal with in one way or another.

But, in taking the factual world seriously, fantasy therapists do not, like the modern secularist mentality, make it all there is to reality. Nor do they reduce the fantasy world to a pale reflection of the fact world. In every instance, they are careful to include both fact and fantasy in their view of "reality." They insist that fantasy has a life and logic of its own. It cannot be demoted to a mere appendage of the fact world. Fantasy helps determine what we consider to be fact just as surely as the other way around. From this perspective, earth is no mere inferior emanation of heaven (as it is in some oriental religions), and heaven is no mere projection of earth (as it is in Marxism or positivism). Both are real.

More importantly, in man himself, the two aspects of total reality are united. Never perfectly, of course, but that is the therapeutic ideal. Here there is even an implicit Christology. In Christian theology Christ is the example of the perfectly fulfilled man, the human being in whom divinity and humanity are fully united. For "fantasy therapy," the mature, creative man combines in himself both the realities (as the classical creeds claim Jesus did), and uses this perfect unity to affirm, recreate, and heal the world (as the New Testament claims Jesus did and all men are called to do).

This theological extrapolation from waking-dream types of therapy also shows why, although we began with Jane Harrison's comment on myth as a starting point in our discussion of religion, we must now question its sufficiency. Christianity, like most religions, utilizes myth, but it is founded on specific historical events. It springs from the lengthy story of the Israelites and the life of a Nazarene peasant. So in our terms, Christianity is and is not a "religion." It is anchored both in the world of fact and in the world of fantasy. Though we would often like to push it one way or another, it remains a stubborn reminder that without both, reality would be the poorer.

Fantasy is essential to human life. For its nourishment and fulfillment it requires "embodiment" in society and history. Rituals, though often perverted, provide the formal structure for freedom and fantasy, and the organ by which fantasy can feed back into the "fact world." Christianity in particular has developed images that facilitate fantasy and the channels by which the fantasy world and the fact world can enrich each other.

Now, however, a word of warning is in order. The preceding discussion of fantasy and faith is in no sense whatever intended as a defense for the brittle heirlooms that now pass for rituals in most churches. Such liturgies serve as perfect examples of what I have called the "ideological distortion" of ritual. They have often deteriorated into techniques by which the group strives to define the consciousness of its members, thwart creativity, and present a phalanx of spurious unity to the world. Ideological rituals, whether of church or state, deserve our scorn.

Idiosyncratic rituals, on the other hand, those pathetic efforts by deritualized moderns to embody fantasy and to find corporate gestures by which feeling can speak—these deserve our sympathy and understanding. It is right that people should be bored or annoyed by the lifeless puppetry of most masses and worship services today. We should be worried if they were not. On the other hand, it may be natural to laugh when we see people in group labs, sensitivity sessions, and social action groups groping for ways to touch, celebrate together, and express the inexpressible. But at least the attempt is there. We should begin at once to disinter the biblical themes from the ecclesiastical tombs in which they have been buried and make them available to fantasy-hungry and ritually emasculated moderns.

And there are two ways to go about this. One is to shake up existing liturgies so that their hidden themes begin to stimulate fantasy and innovation rather than to load us with dead weights. This means nearly reversing the conventional notion of what a ritual is: we should see it not as a content to which people must comply, but as a structure within which they can pulsate and pirouette in unprescribed ways. Ritual should lure people into festive fantasy, put them in touch with the deepest longings of the race, help them to step into the parade of history, and ignite their capacity for creation. Not all rituals will do all this all the time. But given the clammy inanity of what now occurs under the name of liturgy, we should at least remind ourselves occasionally what we have the right to hope for.

The other and perhaps more promising path to living liturgy today is to begin not in the churches but in the world. Start where people seek to celebrate life and hope, and bring as a gift to the feast the Christian themes of festivity. They should never be hauled in and imposed. They are welcome only where they can enliven the festivity, heighten the fantasy, or provide the elements of a liberating structure. Like the images in fantasy therapy, the purpose of Christian themes is not to corral people into doing it our way, but to free them to do their own. Christian dimensions of ritual can add depth, universality, and compassion to secular celebration. They are only properly introduced however, if they unlock, challenge, and reassure. Otherwise they have become ideological nightsticks.

Perhaps one day, if our petrified churchly rituals are cracked open and their buried dimensions exhumed, and if enough ancient insights enrich the festive fantasies of the secular world, the two may find or at least touch each other. Maybe that will be the last day, the day when, as Berdyaev says, the whole world will "dissolve in creative ecstacy."

Fantasy and Utopia

6

Utopia has long been a name for the unreal and the impossible. We have set utopia over against the world. As a matter of fact, it is our utopias that make the world tolerable to us: the cities and mansions that people dream of are those in which they finally live.

—Lewis Mumford, The Story of Utopias

Political Vision

The rebirth of fantasy as well as of festivity is essential to the survival of our civilization, including its political institutions. But fantasy can never be fully yoked to a particular political program. To subject the creative spirit to the fetters of ideology kills it. When art, religion, and imagination become ideological tools they shrivel into caged birds and toothless tigers. However, this does not mean that fantasy has no political significance. Its significance is enormous. This is just why ideologues always try to keep it in harness. When fantasy is neither tamed by ideological leashes nor rendered irrelevant by idiosyncrasy, it can inspire new civilizations and bring empires to their knees.

How? It does so through that particular form of fantasy we might call "utopian thought," social vision, or perhaps simply "political fantasy." Political fantasy goes beyond the mere political imagination. It is not content to dream up interesting twists within existing societal patterns. It envisions new forms of social existence and it operates without first asking whether they are "possible." Utopian thinking is to the *polis,* the corporate human community, what fantasy is to the individual person. It provides the images by which existing societies can be cracked open and recreated. It prevents societies, like thought systems, from becoming "closed and ossified." It can be dangerous if it tempts people away from dealing with the real issues. There are societies that have gone mad in this sense. But a society without the capacity for social fantasy faces equally serious dangers. It will die of sclerosis instead of schizophrenia, a much less interesting way to go.

Like individual fantasy, which needs an open "language" and a vehicle for embodiment if it is not to be lost, political fantasy also requires a symbolism that will stimulate it without constricting it, and a social means both for nourishing it and for feeding its potency back into the polis. Without such a symbolic and structural nexus, political fantasy, like the erratic private visions of individuals, will become incoherent even to its own visionaries, and will soon evaporate into the ozone.

On the other hand political fantasy must never be trapped into those definitions of the possible, the feasible, or the practical that inform any given polis. Like "reality," the term "possibility" is not a very precise one. History has a way of surprising us by confounding our most assured convictions about what is possible. We should not even be too sure about death and taxes. The charge that some idea lacks "realism" can become a spear in the arsenal of reactionaries, hurled testily at anyone whose vision might upset existing privilege and power. Therefore, the powers that be must never hold the mortgage of the house of political fantasy. Its social location must be "in but not of" the existing order. And this is not easy to manage.

In the past a certain type of political fantasy often flourished as what we now call "utopian thought." We find it in the books of Sir Thomas More, Edward Bellamy, Tommaso Campanella, and many others. These venturesome social fantasizers never merely tinkered with rearranging the furniture. They struck out toward a whole new social structure, which they sometimes described in considerable detail. Though some of the contents of their utopias may now strike us as a bit bizarre, their main contribution was to show that man could think out wholesome new social forms. Their influence on the polis has been considerable.

But something has happened to this traditional utopian thinking. It has been declining for two hundred years and by now our society has almost completely lost the capacity for utopian thought. Our images of the future tend to be drawn as extensions of the present. Our social imagination has atrophied. Unlike previous generations whose visions of the society exceeded their means of accomplishing them, we suffer from a surplus of means and a shortage of visions. In this sense we have lost the capacity for fantasy and cannot escape the present. The multihued maps of urban planners rarely include any ideas that are not quantitative extensions of existing cities. Planning institutes project futures that seem woefully similar to the present in most of their characteristics. Even in that bedlam of future speculation, science fiction, the asteroid ages depicted often seem to be marked mainly by vastly expanded and refined technologies. Space travel, telecommunication, robotry, and weapons systems have all been "improved," but rarely does anything significantly new in political terms enter the picture. The most widely read portraits of the future in recent years, *1984* and *Brave New World*, are not utopias at all but "dystopias," warnings to us of how awful things will be if we continue on our present course.

The problem is a serious one. When we run out of images of the future polis that are radically at variance with what we now have, we limit the possible range of changes. We initiate a self-fulfilling prophecy and end up with more of the same. This process soon ends in social and cultural stagnation. It produces the inert society.

In his historical survey of Western man's way of thinking about the future, *The Image of the Future*, Fred L. Polak argues that the main dynamic in Western history has been contributed by images of the future.[1] He suggests that our failure to create new future images can result in what he calls "timeless time," a steady state situation in which innovation applies only to means and no longer to ends.

Why has this happened? Why have we lost our capacity for social self-transcendence? Perhaps the answer is that we have treated utopian thought with the same suspicion and condescension with which we have patronized fantasy. We have marked it down as somehow less respectable than other types of thinking. It is for poets and madmen, not for responsible adults.

In our own recent history we have shot down utopian thinking with a concept that, like "factuality," has become almost a magical amulet. The term is "feasibility." It is a central concept in our current cultural lexicon. Before we launch any new program someone must do a "feasibility study." Those responsible for "feasibility studies" occupy in our time the holy grottos once inhabited by the seers and soothsayers. Shrouded with a mystique of almost preternatural competence, they consult their data banks, computers, and extrapolation techniques. They no longer rely on the gizzards of birds or the patterns of bones dropped from a bag. But their counsel is no less eagerly sought. They are the Delphic oracles of technopolis. Only the foolhardy sets out on an enterprise that has not been pronounced "feasible" by an appropriately ordained consultant.

But what does "feasible" really mean? Shorn of its mystical overtones it merely means possible of accomplishment in view of the social, material, and personal resources now in hand or foreseen. Feasibility thus assumes a future that must grow out of the facts of the present. It discourages our hoping or aspiring toward something that flunks the feasibility test. This limits the sweep of human planning, political action, and cultural innovation. It is the ideology of an inert society.

Although "feasibility" is a watchword especially dear to "systems analysts," there are systems analysts who are not happy about it. One of them, Hasan Ozbekhan, insists that what we think of as "desirable" should always arise from "larger sets of ends than the set that is determined by feasibility alone." This makes the range of choice wider. "A desirable outcome can be imagined and structured in detail," says Ozbekhan in the curious argot of planners, "as an independent conception of the future—independent, that is, from the powerful restrictions that the present imposes." [2] What he means is that we can and should learn how to think in detail about what we *want* without being unduly hampered by the question of *how* we are going to get it. We should allow our means to develop out of our ends, not vice versa.

But how can such imagining be encouraged? How in a realistic, "feasibility"-oriented age can we re-ignite the capacity for sociocultural fantasy? How can we lay hold again of the gift of envisioning radically alternative futures, futures that are neither mere extensions of existing conditions nor choices among options that have been found "feasible" in the light of existing means? This is the primary question. The second is how can the visions we see be injected into the inert body politic without diluting the visions? The answer to the first question has to do with the role of religion in encouraging political fantasy. The answer to the second involves a new definition of the place of the church.

Religion and Political Fantasy

In the past the spinning of visions was one of the functions performed by seers, prophets, and holy men. Of course, religion also thwarted visions as Joan of Arc and many others discovered. The same is true today. Religion often simply legitimates existing institutions, personal styles, and patterns of power distribution. This is religion as the "opiate of the masses." But as Marx rightly saw, religion is not only an *expression* of injustice and suffering; it is also a form of *protest* against it. Often this protest expresses itself in the vision of a new epoch. The political fantasy of a "messianic era," a new age in which the relations of men with each other and with nature are fundamentally transformed, arose quite early in the history of Israel. There are parallels though not equivalents in other religious traditions.

In Christianity this vision of the Kingdom of God or the New Jerusalem has had a rich and stormy career. Sometimes it has acted as a catalyst stimulating the culture to transcend itself and its current values. At other times it has braked and deterred change. It is useful to examine the conditions under which religion operates in these different ways.

The power of the vision of a new world to spark change and innovation is undercut in at least three ways. One is to *postpone* the vision to an epoch beyond time and history. We merely wait for it, and patience becomes a primary virtue. Another way to destroy the catalytic power of a social vision is to *reduce* it to more "realistic" or "feasible" dimensions. We settle for less than we envision because anything more would be utopian. The tension is relaxed. A third is to *spiritualize* or *individualize* the radical hope so much that it becomes trivial, or at least socially inconsequential. The immortality of *my* soul takes the place of a new heaven and a new earth.

All three approaches undermine the political impact of religiously inspired social fantasy. If the new epoch is found only in heaven, in a concordat of compromise, or within my own inner spirit, then social transcendence, at least as inspired by religion, is lost.

How does religion contribute to a society's capacity for self-transcendence? It does so by symbolizing an ideal toward which to strive, and by doing so with enough emotional magnetism to provide a powerful source of motivation. This requires, however, an element of enactment and demonstration— the missing element in most of the classical utopian writers.

There is, however, another utopian tradition in addition to that of More and Campanella. It is the tradition of those who *tried out* new forms of community life and personal human style instead of just writing about them. These are the people who founded Brook Farm and the Oneida Community, people who actually constructed, on a small scale, schools, factories, communities, cities, and regions as a concrete expression of their inspired hopes. They *embodied* political fantasy. And the models they created, though some were bizarre and many were short-lived, often had a powerful influence on the larger body politic.

Today, again, we are beginning to see an outbreak of experiments in new types of human community. Communes and co-ops are appearing all over the country. This new quest is the present form of man's perennial search for the transcendent, the new era, the blessed community. So those who today are patiently groping for new forms of human community, in school, slum, home, and among nations, stand in a long tradition. I do not mean here the tradition of the refugee colonies and immigrant bands who from earliest history have left the larger tribe behind and for one reason or another have split off on their own. There are groups like these. But the ones I mean belong to the ancient company of those who though they are deeply discontented with the state of the society and withdraw at least in part from "the world" to fashion a new communal fabric, never abdicate their responsibility for the whole. They are searching for models that others may learn from.

One important historical example of the conscious reformation of communal life is the Christian monastic movement. It was and is a complex affair and we can make few generalizations about it. However, in a period such as ours, turning again to intentional communities and conscious experimentation with alternative institutional patterns, we might do well to lay aside some of our prejudices about monasticism and look again at its history as a possible source of images for us today.

Let us first dismiss that extremely provincial criticism of monastic life which once sprang from our post-Victorian preoccupation with sexual expression. Because most monks have been celibate we used to dismiss their life styles as unnatural and unattractive. However, only a society trapped in the backlash against nineteenth-century sexual hypocrisy could reduce its judgment of monasticism to these proportions. Already a younger generation of "post-post-Victorians" is appearing for whom sex is not such an issue. The artist Van Gogh perhaps put it best when he said that the sex life of an artist must either be that of a monk or that of a soldier. Anything in between distracts him from his vision. The fact that the monks chose the former should not distract us from their vision.

Monasticism was actually an immense and multifarious series of experiments in alternative community life styles. The monks prayed and meditated (directed fantasy), sang, read, composed music, copied and illuminated manuscripts, studied every classical language and discipline, developed new agricultural techniques, provided solace and hospitality, worked, ate, and drank together in thousands of different communal patterns. Nor were they wholly "withdrawn" from the everyday world. They interacted with it at a hundred different levels. They served, taught, nursed, prayed for, and contributed to the life of the commonweal. The different monastic orders embodied numberless fantasies of how human beings could live together in love and mutuality.

The monks understood their relation to the rest of Christendom within a theological worldview that seems implausible to us today, at least on the surface. They were praying for the people who had less time to pray because they fought, ruled, or toiled in the fields. The monks lived out a longing for spiritual perfection that was hardly possible for all men. Their communities, in other words, were contributing in their own distinctive way to the future everyone in Christendom expected or at least hoped for, a blissful reward in heaven after death.

Though this theology eludes us today, the monks were really more accurate than we often think. They were in fact contributing to the future of the whole civilization, though not quite in the way they understood. The seeds of the Renaissance and the Reformation were cultivated in the monasteries. Luther and Mendel were both monks. The Benedictines practiced participatory democracy centuries before it became a political issue. The idea of a disciplined work schedule and of work as service to God began with the monks, and without it the whole Industrial Revolution could never have occurred. Max Weber was right when he said that during the Reformation "every man became a monk and the whole world a monastery." Life styles, discipline, and communal patterns that had been born, nourished, and refined in small communities now supplied the pattern for a whole civilization.

Many monasteries were closed during the Reformation. But the tradition of model human communities acting out their visions of human life did not die. Utopian communities began to spring up and the practice continues down to our day. During the sixteenth century whole cities such as Geneva and Münster became the sites of model communities. Often property was shared, as the monks had done it, and in some places so were wives and children. In general, the more visionary of these experiments, now grouped by scholars under the term "radical Reformation," were uprooted and destroyed by Lutheran, Catholic, and Calvinist authorities. The ideas lived on, however, and American history is studded with examples of communitarian utopias, from Oneida to California's new rural communes.

Today we are witnessing a rebirth of the monastic, utopian tradition. It is good that we are. A society needs seedplots and models. It needs a variety of experimental tryouts of new institutions, life patterns, values, symbols, and rituals. Not all of these will survive and only a few will ever see their visions incorporated by the larger *polis*. The medieval period saw the birth of hundreds of monastic movements that split, expired, or disappeared, but others survived to enrich the entire epoch.

The new monasticism we need will, of course, differ from the old in a number of ways. It can hardly be built around vows of celibacy, although it must be said that these vows did serve a real purpose once. So many later utopian communities have foundered on sex we are forced to concede that the ability of some monasteries to survive for centuries may have had something to do with the "monk's solution" to this perennial problem. The Oneida group tried out a form of group marriage. Present utopian communities are evolving still newer ways of dealing with sex, children, and family structure. It is good that they are. We cannot merely assume that the present urban nuclear family will continue forever.

Also, model communities must find some way to grasp and symbolize their relation to the whole that avoids both the arrogant abdication of "humaner than thou" withdrawal as well as the servility of the research team that strays only as far as the corporation allows it. Here, the monastic model, in which the oneness of Christendom still operated as a unifying theme, is more helpful than the extreme Protestant sectarian idea in which sometimes each schismatic group claimed that it alone was *vera ecclesia christi.* We need a theology of political fantasy that will undergird conflict, unflinching criticism, radically variant values, and very disparate corporate patterns since eventually all these will be salutary for the whole. This perspective must be shared in some measure by the highly variegated experimental communities themselves and by the "straight" civilization of which they are still a part.

Finally, in our time, it will be necessary for utopian experimentation to innovate in only one aspect of a society's whole life. Some people, of course, may still be able to enter fully into total subsocieties where education, worship, work, and play are all included. Most, however, will live part of their lives in the "straight" world of facts and feasibility, and will be involved in the continuous embodiment of political fantasy in only one or two aspects of life—in their leisure, residence, politics, schooling, worship, or work. This requirement stems from the multiplex structure of our urban society. We are sorted out into such a variety of functional relations—at school, club, office, home—that we are able to experiment, perhaps even quite radically, with one without needing to wait until the others are ready to come along. This enables visionaries to project and act out their fantasies in one sector without feeling they must transform everything at once. A person can participate in a wholly new kind of educational, familial, or housing concept without breaking his relation to the electric company or even the city government.

Johannes Metz, a Roman Catholic theologian, has rightly insisted that there is a valid place for ascetic discipline and monasticism today, even for a "flight from the world." However, this flight must be, he says, a "Flucht nach vorn," a conscious movement *ahead*, into the future.[3] It must grow out of an ascetical refusal to be bound by today's societal standards, a bold attempt to shape the future of human community by stepping toward that future before it engulfs us.

Rabelais, in his *Gargantua and Pantagruel,* draws a fetching portrait of the fictional Abbey of Theleme where under the escutcheon "Do As You Please," people gathered away from the diversions of the world to pursue enjoyment in single-minded devotion. Historians of the utopian movement believe the idea of the Abbey of Theleme was an enormously important one for the model communities men hatched later. The exotic fantasy of Rabelais had succeeded by using a traditional form, the abbey, to convey a different content. Again structure facilitated both fantasy and its feedback.

The Abbey of Theleme can hardly serve as our model now. Nor can Münster or Brook Farm. But here and there all over the world today venturesome people are beginning to experiment with brazen new forms of human interaction. The search for "transcendence" is not dead today. It takes the form of the quest for livelier, more just, more satisfying, and gentler forms of human community. It continues that seeking after the ever future Kingdom that Jesus commended. What these various experiments need is not a common ideology, but a way to understand each other, a stimulus to keep going and a circuiting through which the energy they generate can vitalize the rest of us.

In the medieval period the genius of a universal church managed to include both model communities and the larger society in one catholic family. After the Reformation, though the institutional unity was broken, schismatic sectarians and orthodox churchmen at least shared the common symbols of Christianity. Even people intent on burning each other were tuned in on the same symbolic signal.

Today, however, we have no common wave length to keep us in touch. Nor do we have an institution that somehow makes St. Francis understandable to the Emperor, and allows peasants, priests, monks, and knights all to see some sense in the calling of the other. Today our conscious community experimenters are out of touch, symbolically and institutionally, not only with the *polis* but with each other.

We cannot return to the medieval wave length, nor should we desire to. That period paid a high price for its unity and its capacity for communication. The vitalities of history finally cracked it open. What we can ask, however, is whether we today can have a structure that will both energize and legitimate social fantasy, and which will permit a playback of fantasy without imposing preconceived limits on what is to be dreamed.

The Church as Experimental Community

We live at a time when all our inherited institutions from the family and the university to the nation state and the system of international trade are under question. There is not a single institution that we take for granted. Not only that, but the authority structures of all institutions are caving in. Vertical bureaucracies are collapsing. Inherited privilege cuts very little ice. Increasingly people exert authority only because they can make a contribution to some shared purpose.

But just because our inherited institutions are cracking and splintering does not mean we have new ones ready to take their places. Maybe we should not. Maybe the patterns that emerge from the disintegration of existing institutions will differ so markedly from our present ones that we should not even call them "institutions." That question remains open.

Whatever happens, however, people will continue to dream up new and different ways of living together. They will have to. The pace of change always reveals the inadequacy of existing ways, and that pace is accelerating. People will not only dream up new patterns and be criticized for doing so. They will try them out on a small scale, refine them, discard some, keep others. If their activity ever ceases human society will rumble to a stop, rust, and disintegrate. Just as individuals need a fantasy life to keep alive, societies need fantasy to survive. Political fantasy, the fantasy of the *polis*, is not a luxury but a necessity.

But political fantasy cannot proceed in a vacuum. It requires a "field," a symbolic and structural context. It needs a special form of flexible institution in order to live and to interact creatively with the political world. This must be an institution that has the form of an ordinary institution, but that differs because it exists not for itself but to link the two worlds of fact and fantasy. Let us call it a "metainstitution." This "metainstitution" must have a number of characteristics. In order to animate fantasy it must cultivate the symbols that opened men to new levels of awareness in the past. It must be in effective touch with the most advanced artistic movement of the day and with historical and transhistorical images of the future. It must teach men to celebrate and fantasize. But above all it must provide a fertile field where new symbols can appear. Since man is body and heart as well as brain, it must include affective and ritual components. Finally, it must be a part of the culture in which it lives but sufficiently free so that its fantasies are not pinioned and hamstrung by present expectations.

To move to traditional theological language for a moment, this metainstitution must be one in which the lives of the prophets and saints of old are commemorated, in which the hope for the New Humanity is celebrated and in which "new truths" are "ever breaking forth from God's holy word." It must be a polis within the polis, living within the political community but neither identical with it nor slavishly loyal to it. It must be a pilgrim band that has no earthly home, but seeks "another city," whose king is not Caesar.

This, of course, is language traditionally used about the church. Can this needed metainstitution be the church? The very idea sounds preposterous, and is. But the fact that we so quickly reject the notion is a dismal commentary on how far the institutional church has strayed from its historical calling. The church more often than not uses the memories of the saints not to encourage us in creativity but to bludgeon us into conformity. It has emptied the gestures of celebration until they have become barren and joyless. It has discouraged radical fantasy as a possible threat to its hard-won place in Caesar's society. It cannot take the risk of putting its ultimate loyalty in the "world to come" (the tomorrow of embodied fantasy), because it has too deep a stake in the world of yesterday and today.

The sad truth is that the church *cannot* be the metainstitution our world needs to instruct us in festivity, to open us to fantasy, to call us to tomorrow, or to enlarge our petty definitions of reality. It cannot for only one reason: the church is not the church. That is, what we now call "churches" have departed so markedly from their vocation as agents and advocates of Christian faith that only a residue of that historic calling remains. Dim echoes of it are still heard in its preaching and pale shadows of it appear in its liturgy. But the substance has been thinned and the spirit dulled.

The breach between what the churches were meant to be and what they have become is almost as wide as the chasm between what they now are and the saving remnant our world needs. For this reason that familiar question, "Can our present churches be renewed so that they can assume their real task?" is not the basic one.

The question we should be asking should run like this: Given the fact that our polis, the human community, needs a company of dreamers, seers, servants, and jesters in its midst, where shall this company come from? Given the fact that biblical imagery—Jesus, Job, Jeremiah—has produced prophets and revolutionaries in the past, how can we keep telling these stories? Given the fact that in festive ritual man's fantasy life is both fed and kept in touch with the earth, how can we eat the bread and toast the hope in ways that ring true? How can we keep restating the vision of the New Age so that the poor and the persecuted continue to push and the princes and potentates never feel secure?

When we ask these questions we are no closer to satisfying answers, perhaps. But at least we have stopped restricting our vision. Worrying about what might be possible in the existing churches is fruitless. By changing the question we have moved from mere ecclesiastical imagination to the level of true fantasy. We have left behind the tired and useless task of "renewing the church" and are now concerned with the recreation of the world.

Then, surprisingly perhaps, when we are no longer fixated on their "renewal," we may begin to notice aspects of the churches that can contribute to that coming metainstitution of festivity and fantasy we need and want. We can detect life beneath the crust and embers in the ashes. Here and there a small flame may even break through. Nevertheless, the new church we look for need not come entirely from the churches of today. It certainly will not. It will come, if it comes at all, as a new congeries of elements, some from the churches, some from outside, some from those fertile interstices between. And it will assume a shape we can hardly predict, though we can sometimes see its outlines—in fantasy.

Part Three

Mystics and Militants 7

Thou shalt not be on friendly terms
With guys in advertising firms,
  Nor speak with such
As read the Bible for its prose,
Nor, above all, make love to those
  Who wash too much.

—W. H. Auden, "Under Which Lyre? A Reactionary Tract for the Times"

The forces that bear the seeds of a renewal of festivity and fantasy in our time are not apt to come from the churches alone. This chapter is devoted to two such movements, which both splashed into view in the late 1960's. Both are extraordinarily important for the future. Both are theologically fascinating. Let us call them the *neomystics* and the *new militants*.

The neomystics, mostly white, in bells and beads, came on with love-ins in the park, chanted mantras, and smoked pot. The new militants, both black and white, with beards and bull-horns, staged sit-ins in university administration buildings, blockaded Dow recruiters, and picketed induction centers. Both scared and bewildered folks over thirty. Both sparked new hope in those who had given up on anything fresh ever happening again in America. Both sometimes did things that worried even their most fervent devotees. Yet together they represent two insights that have immeasurable significance for the whole society.

The insight of the neomystics is that the search for the holy —perhaps even the quest for God—is important after all, and that it is integrally tied up with the search for an authentically human style of life. Despite secularization, mysticism is back again, and with it a new interest in ritual, contemplation, and even in visions. The insight of the new militants is that politics is not dead and that in fact every act has an irreduceable political significance. A period of social activism rivaled only by the 1930's is in full swing. Radical rhetoric is on the wing and the term revolution is once again heard in the land.

The groups that represent these insights have been referred to variously as "hippies" or flower children on the one hand, and "the new left" on the other. By now, however, these terms have been applied so indiscriminately and with such prejudicial overtones that I prefer to use different ones. The term "neo-mystic" is better. "Mystic" indicates the ancient tradition from which the new interest springs; at the same time the prefix "neo" suggests there is something novel about it. The same is true for the new militants. To describe them with the label "left" is misleading because it places them in terms of categories they themselves believe to be outdated. Yet they must certainly be understood in the light of the tradition of political militancy that has played such an important role in Western history in the past three centuries. But labeling is not really an important problem. The real question is what is the long-term religious and political significance of these two movements?

The Neomystics: Festivity and Contemplation

Today's new mystics represent a modern phase in a very old religious movement. They personify man's ancient thirst to taste both the holy and the human with unmediated directness. Like previous generations of mystics, the new ones suspect all secondhand reports. Also they wish to lose themselves, at least temporarily, in the reality they experience. Above all, like the mystics of old, when they try to tell us what they are up to, we have a hard time understanding them. Mystics speak a language of their own, and sometimes even their fellow mystics do not quite get the message.

The neomystics, unlike many of the old ones, luxuriate in loud music, bright costumes, and convulsive dancing. Still, they are right when they use the word "contemplative" to describe their way of life. We are confused because to many people "contemplative" is associated with soft music, black costumes, and vows of celibacy and obedience. How then can the sportive, sometimes even self-indulgent, life of the neomystics be called contemplative?

"Contemplation" means different things to different people. At its narrowest, it suggests a discipline for achieving a particular state of consciousness. In this restricted sense, techniques of contemplation have been refined for years, especially by the great Christian mystics such as Jacob Boehme and St. John of the Cross and by the rich mystical traditions of the East.

In its wider sense, however, as suggested both by some of the classical Western mystics and as emphasized in Zen Buddhism, contemplation is a total way of life. It is a basic attitude toward all things, including detachment, perspective, and an element of irony. According to this broader view, the contemplative life may require periods of withdrawal and the use of established techniques of meditation in some stages, but basically it is a life that can be lived anywhere. It is a way of being, a style of existence.

In both senses of the word, contemplation bears a striking resemblance to festivity. Carl Kerényi asserts this similarity when he says in one of his books, that celebrating a festival is the equivalent to becoming contemplative, and "in this state, directly confronting the higher realities on which the whole of existence rests." [1] What Kerényi is driving at is that festivity allows us to remove our attention from everyday pursuits and direct it to the immediate festive experience of joy, appreciation, and anticipation. Further, festivity resembles contemplation, because it is not just a means to something else. It is an end in its own right. Also in line with other contemplative disciplines, festivity requires an element of sacrifice or renunciation. We cannot really celebrate if we are getting paid for it, which is why professional mourners and paid-escort services strike us as a bit phoney. We celebrate best when we joyfully give up the time involved and wantonly accept the fact that celebrating is not an economically productive activity.

Festivity and contemplation are close cousins. The things that make life contemplative are the same things that make life celebrative: the capacity to step back from tasks and chores, the ability to "hang loose" from merely material goals, the readiness to relish an experience on its own terms. It was the much-criticized, exploited, and now virtually defunct "hippie" movement that helped our chore-ridden society to notice this. For that contribution they deserve the society's gratitude, not its reprobation.

So mysticism is back in our midst and, as always, many people view it with mixed emotions. It has always been thus with mystics. Traditionally religious people are glad on the one hand that mystics want to find God. They are bothered, on the other, that the mystics are not satisfied with existing ecclesiastical means of grace. Besides, in their single-minded quest for the holy vision, mystics are likely to offend prevailing social sensibilities. Mysticism is not always serene and placid. It can become noisy, Dionysiac, even orgiastic. It has little use for institutional religion. So organized religions, with good reason, have usually been nervous about mystics, and they remain so today. In our present situation, this perennial suspicion is deepened because of the means some neomystics employ to celebrate or contemplate. I refer especially to the growing use of psychedelic drugs and of elaborately contrived multimedia "mind-blowing" environments. Though this subject is a large one, no discussion of mysticism and festivity today would be complete without some mention of it.

Pipes and Bowls

Lubricating festivity with spirits, potions, and additives is scarcely a new idea. Intoxicating drinks appeared in man's life at the very dawn of history.[2] They have played a role in religious rites since then. Wine is used in communion services, and in secular festivities; the punch bowl or the brimming beaker still occupies a central place. But are we not aware of the immense dangers involved in misusing alcohol? Many people are. Some still are not. But in any case we seem to have rejected total abstinence as a viable solution. Today, instead of abstinence pledges, we try to teach young people to enjoy drinking, to experience it as a normal part of life, and to discover their own limits.[3] We even tolerate drinking to slight excess on some occasions. We have not solved the serious problem of alcoholism, and we need to think about it more than we do. But we have decided, as a society, that we will have to solve it by learning to live with alcohol, not without it.

We drink alcohol not just because we like its taste but because it produces a certain state of consciousness. Nor is our society particularly opposed to inducing other desired states of consciousness (or unconsciousness) with substances in addition to alcohol. We quaff caffeine to cajole our brains into awakening in the morning. We drag on a pipe to relax. We order a martini to help clinch a business deal or madeira to speed a seduction. We pop a Sleep-eze or sip warm cocoa to encourage slumber. But when it comes to the well-publicized drugs now increasingly used by young people, we suddenly turn angry and petulant. We serve champagne at wedding receptions but put people behind bars for smoking marijuana.

Why? There seems to be no really convincing reason. Certainly what medical knowledge we have of alcohol and marijuana would not support such wildly disproportionate attitudes. But in this confused and emotion-packed area, reason seems to have little place. Our whole approach to stimulants, depressants, psychedelic drugs and hallucinogens today is a quagmire of irrationality, prejudice, and inconsistency. We unthinkingly lump hard and soft, addictive and nonaddictive substances together under the scare word "dope." We list marijuana with heroin as though both belong in the same bin. We have created a panicky atmosphere that makes careful, controlled research in the new synthetic drugs like LSD virtually impossible. Consequently wild stories, abuse, and sensationalism have run amuck, and rational discussion of the issue seems impossible for the moment.

We need a period of calm in which the reasoned investigation of various drugs can proceed. We need a moratorium both on flamboyant drug cults and well-publicized "busts" so that real evidence can be accumulated on the benefits and dangers of the various substances now in use. Can anything be said in the meantime?

First, it would help if we understood that we labor under an obvious cultural bias. Recently a middle-aged Catholic priest who had grown up in Yugoslavia confessed to me that he really did not understand what all the fuss was about. As a lad, he had lived in a village that was half Catholic and half Moslem. The Catholics, although permitted to drink alcohol, were absolutely forbidden to smoke hashish. The Moslems were prohibited by their faith from drinking liquor but felt no qualms about smoking the sweet grass. As boys always do, the youngsters from different sides of town would creep with their friends into each other's back rooms to taste the forbidden fruit. There the Moslem boys would savor the piquant *slivovitz* and the Catholics would steal a puff on the *hookah*.

Though phrased in religious terms, the prohibitions were obviously cultural and very relative. Whatever attitudes we eventually develop on drugs should not be a product of mere social prejudice. They should be based on a realistic assessment of what alcohol, marijuana, caffeine, nicotine, and all the rest can or cannot do for us or to us. This is a field that badly needs demythologizing. Extravagant claims and charges should be held in abeyance until more clinical data has been assembled and verified.

The time may come when we will recognize that the various substances we smoke, swallow, or swill to induce particular states of consciousness are all devices that in a perfect world of fulfilled human beings, no one would need. But no one lives in such a world. We are beset by noise, interruptions, and banal chores. We sometimes want to contemplate or celebrate, but the world is too much with us. So we use the substances nature has placed in the grains and grasses. Often we misuse them. But the fact that something is misused does not mean it should be banned. If it did, money, sex, and printing presses would have to join wine and marijuana on the index of prohibited items.

What we need now are dependable data on just how much harm any of these substances can do to people. We know a good deal about the harm that cigarettes and whiskey can cause. We know about the damaging effects of heroin and cocaine. We do not know enough about marijuana and very little about the so-called psychedelics. We do know that many people insist that liquor helps them to relax, or that pot helps them meditate, or that either one helps them celebrate. We need to find out what else these things may be doing—not so that we can pile up massive repressive legislation, but so that people can make choices on facts instead of on the reports of terrified high school teachers or self-designated gurus. Mead bowls, magic mushrooms, and peace-pipes have been with mankind for many millennia. It is unlikely that they will disappear very soon, if ever. What we can hope for, however, is that human beings will learn to use them with a mature recognition of their benefits, their dangers, and their limits.

Above all, we should learn never to confuse real festivity with mere intoxication. Authentic festivity can never be cooked up with pharmacological catalysts. Nor does their absence prevent its arrival. The spirit of festivity, like a muse, has a mind of its own. It can fail to show up even when elaborate preparations have been made, leaving us all feeling a little silly. It may pop in when no one is expecting it. In this respect, it reminds us of the grace of God, unmerited and often unanticipated. It cannot simply be turned on and off at will.

Still, sometimes preparation for festivity does pay off. As Sister Corita Kent says, if you ice a cake, light sparklers and sing, something celebrative may happen. Also, if we seriously practice contemplative disciplines that have been developed over the centuries, we may have a better chance of discovering the significance of meditation.

The Multimedia Environment

There is a striking difference between the hermit's cell of the old style mystic and the festive settings created by our neo-mystics today. The contrast is so vivid that it forces us to ask again whether we are not dealing here with very different, even contradictory phenomena. We have tried to demonstrate a similarity between festivity and contemplation. But what does the solemn quietude and serenity of the classical mystic's cave have in common with the strobe lights and triple fortissimo music of a multimedia environment? Do these two not occupy opposite poles on the spectrum?

Opposite yes, but perhaps sufficiently opposite to approach each other and to share certain important similarities. Many classical mystics tried to reach their goal through sensory deprivation. A drab cell reduced optical stimulation to a minimum. Silence, plain clothes, and meager food minimized other sensory inputs. Deprived of its normal diversions, the consciousness was free to focus on something else. The intense multimedia environment strives for the same effect with different means. Instead of reaching a threshold of consciousness through sensory deprivation, it relies on sensory overload. It induces a different dimension of awareness, not by depriving the senses of stimuli, but by pounding the senses with so many inputs and at such speed that the normal sorting mechanisms cannot cope. It recalls the "pandemonium" of the ancient rites of Dionysus, rites which were one of the sources of Greek drama.

Take the effect of a flashing strobe light, for example. Much in use today in multimedia events, the strobe light interrupts the smooth flow of visual images and chops them into shredded instants. Every second now requires a new "take." But because our eyes and brains cannot function quickly enough to sort and classify each separate instant, we stop trying and begin to let the images flow in unsorted. We learn for the moment to float along passively on our visual perceptions without trying to master or arrange them. We may even get some feeling for the outer limits and precariousness of the visual experience itself. Now compare this to Josef Pieper's description of that experience which has sometimes been called "speculation." It means, he says, "to look at reality purely receptively—in such a way that things are the measure and the soul is exclusively receptive." [4] In both cases a period of venturesome openness to experience replaces our usual guarded and suspicious attitude.

Multiple sound and light sources have a similar effect. They make it impossible for us to put all our perceptions together in an integrated whole. Since too much is happening to permit the classification of everything into existing modes of awareness, the patterns of meaning we generally bring to experience must be temporarily suspended. The effect is quite accurately described by the phrase, "mind-blowing." Our habitual reading of reality is set aside and new dimensions of awareness can appear. Also, when music is really loud, so loud that it totally occupies our aural capacities, we experience something curiously akin to deep and pervasive silence.

All this suggests that disciplined sensory deprivation as experienced by the classical mystics, and the modern experience of calculated sensory overload do produce some markedly similar results. This in turn supports the notion that noisy festivity and silent contemplation may not be as different as they first appear.

But like any other human creation, the catalytic environment cannot produce God at man's beck and call. It represents the contemporary technological equivalent of the pageants, feasts, and bonfires men have staged since the dawn of consciousness. It is subject to the same elements of promise and possibility and open to the same abuse. Multimedia blow-outs can and do deteriorate into mere sensory orgies. Like pageants and celebrations from time immemorial they require delicacy and discipline to make them occasions for authentic human growth. Above all they must be directed toward dimensions of experience and symbols that lead us *into* historical existence and freedom.

This is where the religious dimension of celebration enters. Christianity has nothing against noise and revelry as such. It does suggest, however, that celebration should open man not just to the joy of his senses and the élan of the feast itself, but to the larger cosmos of which he is a part and the history he is involved in making. Real celebration links us to a world of memories, gestures, values, and hopes that we share with a much larger community. This may shed light on the real meaning of that phrase from the Christian communion service which rings so strangely in our modern ears:

> *Therefore with Angels and*
> *Archangels, and with all the company of heaven . . .*

The "Angels and Archangels" symbolize poetically those marvelous dimensions of reality we touch only in celebration and fantasy. The "company of heaven" linked to those of us on earth suggests that very large and inclusive human community of which I become a conscious part in celebration.

Man becomes man only when he knows and feels himself within a larger drama, one he not only acts in but helps to create. Even the most elaborately planned festivity can never guarantee this to anyone. But since he first stood up on two legs, and perhaps before, man has celebrated. He probably always will. Our challenge today is to deepen and enliven this celebration so that it becomes an occasion for nourishing our most courageous hopes and saluting the biggest tribe of all.

Maybe that is why something seems absent from the festivity of the neomystics. It is often a celebration of celebration. What is missing is that toasting of historical event and social hope that would give the festivity political significance. Here the issue is basically a theological one. In Christian and Jewish festivals, people celebrate historical events and concrete hopes. The gritty confusion of earthly history provides the principal focus of God's being, so festivity is always inherently political whether one wants it to be or not. By elevating and expressing **hopes for things which have not yet come to be, this kind of** festivity always produces friction in society.

So far for most of the neomystics the rediscovery of celebration, though inventive and colorful, often remains nonhistorical and therefore nonpolitical. It can even be an escape from politics. Man cannot celebrate abstractions, so the celebration of "love" and "peace" dissolves into frivolity unless it becomes more particular. People do not celebrate "love" but the love of John for Mary. Nor do we celebrate "freedom," but the liberation of the Israelites from Egypt or of black people from modern bondage. Christianity and Judaism have a definite bias for persons and events rather than for minds and ideas. This supplies the tension point at which Christianity may most fruitfully interact with the neomystics. It should welcome the verve and brightness they incarnate. But it should help them transform celebration into a way of being *in* the world, not a way of getting out of it.

Inspired by their gurus and holy men, the young people of today are fashioning their own celebrations and rituals. Rock music, guerrilla theatre, Dionysian dance, projected light and color—all play a part in the evolving rites. This is also true among the growing number of political activists. Unlike those of the "old left" who despised all forms of religion as the opiate of the masses, the new radicals exhibit a pervasive interest in theological questions and even in such occult topics as astrology and clairvoyance. So far the religious rebirth among young people is in a state of brawling, turbulent infancy. As it develops its rituals, however, it will inevitably fall prey to the same dangers that stalk any religious movement. Its rituals could become oppressive and ideological, a flashy set of devices for herding people into this or that action. Or its rituals could fall into eccentric fragments and therefore fail to unite people in celebration. The challenge Christianity faces is how to embrace this spiritual renaissance without crushing it, how to enrich it without polluting it, how to deepen it without mutilating it. Whether the current religious awakening can be saved from its own worst excesses depends on how it manages to relate itself to history, and to politics.

The Militant: Politics and Imagination

If the neomystics hunger for a truly human personal life, the new militants thirst for a society in which everyone has a real share in creating the future. If the key word for the mystics is "contemplation," for the militants it is "participation." The militants have caught the vision of man as a subject, not just an object, in the political process. They insist that not just minds but institutions must be "blown" and remade if we are ever to have a participative society.

The new militants, like the neomystics, represent a contemporary chapter in an old story. They are the spiritual descendants of the social visionaries and utopian radicals of the past. They are not satisfied with present definitions of what is "real" and what is "possible." As put by one of their theorists, Herbert Marcuse, they want to "break the power of facts over the world and to speak a language which is not the language of those who establish, enforce, and benefit from the facts." [5]

Though they are often unaware of it, the new militants personify a way of thinking that goes back at least as far as the early messianic hopes of Israel. The capacity not to take present "reality" as final springs from a confidence that a better reality is not only desirable but possible. In ancient Israel, this confidence took the form of the belief in a coming messianic era where the lion would lie down with the lamb, and men would study war no more. In the Christian era this conviction led the early followers of Jesus to view the colossal and allegedly eternal Roman empire not as a fixed reality they had to adjust to, but as something marked for extinction. They were not interested in doctoring up the "system," but in preparing for a superior reality that was going to replace it.

For many centuries, Christians assumed a very passive role toward the coming new heaven and new earth. It would come when God was ready. Beginning with small groups during the medieval period however, and culminating in the Radical Reformation in the sixteenth century, this patient attitude underwent a fundamental change. Now some Christians decided that they should not just wait and pray for the coming new era but should actively seek to bring it about. The abortive peasants' revolt of the early sixteenth century sprang from this new conviction. The fact that subsequent Western revolutions often became anticlerical and anti-Christian should not be allowed to obscure the source of the original impetus. The belief that present political structures need not be taken with ultimate seriousness and that a new reality is possible springs originally from biblical faith. The fact that Christianity has so often in its history become counterrevolutionary betrays a drastic deviation from its sources. The radical utopian tradition in politics, however secularized it may recently have become, is an offspring of religion. In trying to understand the new militants this is an important fact to remember. Perhaps the best way to uncover the style and significance of the new militants is to compare and contrast them with the neomystics we have just described.

At one level the similarity is quite striking. It is a concern for the human person. Behind the beads and the "be-ins," the real point the neomystics are making is a simple one. They contend that we human beings owe ourselves more time to do humanly significant things. In their opinion, we are all zombies enslaved by little black datebooks. Our calendars push and squeeze us until we have no time to feel, make love, delight in the beauty of the world, smell flowers, play. We are all too uptight and money-mad. But here there comes an important difference. For the flower people there is no need to struggle for power. The society is putrified within and will soon topple of its own accord. The only sensible tactic is to leave behind the collapsing edifice of Western culture and get far enough away from it, geographically if possible, but at least psychologically, so as not to be bruised by the debris when it falls. So, like the first Franciscans, they walk the streets in happy poverty conversing with the birds and angering the sensible, thrifty pillars of the society. Or, like the desert fathers of early Christian history, they flee to the caves and fields to preserve what they believe is valuable in the face of the imminent collapse of civilization.

For the politically active militants the sickness of society is also its authoritarian repressiveness. But they see the squeeze more in the hoarded power of greedy elites cutting people off from decision-making and thus from the privileges and benefits of life. As the phrase "participatory democracy" suggests, the activists want to redistribute decision-making so that more and more people, especially the black, the poor, and the young, will have some control over their own futures. For these new militants, the institutions of society are not about to collapse, but are becoming more entrenched. Their tactic, therefore, is not withdrawal but confrontation. Instead of "turn on and drop out," they prefer to sit in and take over.

Thus there are important differences between the neomystics and the new militants. The mystics accuse the militants of fighting the same old battle for power instead of moving on to a new level of consciousness where none of that really matters anymore. The new left activists see the flower people at best as childlike and immature, at worst as self-indulgent escapists, concerned more for the state of their perception than they are for the victims of napalm and roaches.

But these two groups also have a good deal in common, especially in contrast to the larger culture that both criticize so vehemently. Both agree that a fundamental change is needed in society and that such a change cannot be accomplished merely through normal political channels. Both strongly emphasize the inner voice of conscience as the final arbiter in moral affairs. So the differences between the two groups, though substantial, should not be overemphasized. It is probably even inaccurate to designate them as "groups," since there are important points at which the two streams mix and intermingle.

Nor should we make the mistake of trying to understand the neomystics and the new militants merely as reactions against our society. In part they are. But they may be signs as well as symptoms, the most visible surface ripples rising from tidal movements that will eventually change the contours of our whole civilization. If this is so, then it is important to examine the other side of the ledger for the possible danger they reflect, not as critics of our society, but as symptoms of its malaise.

Violence and the "Cop-Out"

Corresponding to these two vital discoveries of the neomystics and the new militants, there lurk in our time two deadly temptations. These are the temptation of *violence* on the one side, and of the *"cop-out"* on the other.

What do these terms mean? I am not a pacifist, so when I speak of violence, I do not mean to condemn the use of force unconditionally. There are situations, as even Pope Paul VI conceded in his encyclical *Populorum progressio*, in which oppressed groups have no other recourse. By "violence" I am not referring merely to the use of force, but to the use of force on an unnecessary scale in situations where other effective means could still be used. Nor by "cop-out" do I mean those short, or extended, periods of standing back from the fray we all need occasionally. The "cop-out" is the pursuit of merely personal or small group ends to the exclusion of any continuing interest in societal issues. It is an abdication of membership in the larger human commonwealth.

On the fringes of the new militants, black and white, there are people who have succumbed to the mystique of violence. On the "flower power" scene, there are many more who have drifted into near-total withdrawal. But these two groups by no means contain the major violent or copped-out segments of the society. The violence of the military and the "environmental violence" inflicted on the ghetto by landlords, police, and the welfare system far exceed the puny violence displayed so far in colonial revolts and urban uprisings. Also, withdrawal is not the monopoly of hippies. The retreat of middle-class Americans into their zoned Xanadus and moated suburbs makes their criticism of the hippies sound very hollow. In fact the cop-out of the rich and powerful from their responsibilities in the society is a form of violence just as surely as the violence of the assassin is a copping-out from the accepted procedures human beings should use to contend with each other.

The retreat to violence and the cop-out are similar, and they are the temptations not only of some young people but of the total society. Perhaps what our whole era needs is a vision of personal fulfillment that will not lead us to cop-out and a vision of the polis that will save us from destroying ourselves and others in our quest for human justice. Here the neomystics and the new militants need each other, and we all need them both. The only man who can save the world today must be a mixture of the saint and the revolutionary. He must be a mixture, that is, of the mystic and the militant. But how can these ingredients be combined?

Politics, Contemplation, and Festivity

During the early spring of 1968, in a populous eastern city, a troubled young man came to a difficult decision. His application for the status of a conscientious objector had been turned down by his draft board. Having exhausted all other alternatives, he finally decided he could not accept induction into the army. To dramatize his stand, and his willingness to accept the consequences, he determined to do what he had seen some of his friends do already—to report to the induction center but not to take the symbolic step forward. However, on previous occasions he had noticed that such acts of conscience were always accompanied by a high degree of fear and hostility, not only on the part of the officials at the induction center and the other inductees, but also among those sympathetic to the refusal. The whole occasion had often deteriorated into something ugly and destructive. This young man determined that when he reported, the atmosphere would be different.

It was. Laying his plans far in advance, he asked his girl-friend to bring along fresh-baked bread and strawberry jam. Balloons, flowers, and banners were arranged for. A rock-and-roll band volunteered its services. As a result, the scene at the induction center was one of celebration and color, a miniature "be-in."

In the midst of the life-affirming atmosphere of bright mini-skirts and fresh blossoms, even those deeply opposed to induction refusal seemed more understanding. In this case the "no" to an unjust war was expressed firmly but as a minor note in the major theme of saying "yes" to life and peace. At that moment festivity brought the most authentic insights of the young anti-war militants and the mystical flower children together. The atmosphere it engendered even included, in part at least, those who violently disagree with both.

Why did festivity afford such a powerful link? Because it released the main positive contribution of both. On the one hand, festivity in its essence is very close to the mysticism, immediacy, and contemplation that are the major concerns of the flower people. On the other hand, festivity is in its very essence participatory and antiauthoritarian, two central values of the political radicals.

During a fiesta, as Octavio Paz says in his book on Mexico,[6] the ranks and stations of life are violated. We poke fun at the army, the law, the church. We flagrantly violate the authoritative hierarchies of life. We pretend for a moment that we live in that free, nonoppressive world of our hopes and fantasies. We resurrect the Feast of Fools.

Also, at a celebration, we want everyone to take part. We dislike wallflowers, party-poopers, cliques. A festival seems successful only when everyone has imbibed its spirit. If someone is left out, everyone feels the worse for it. Thus, the very essence of celebration is participation and equality, the abolition of domination and paternalism.

No doubt what the new militants need more than anything else is a heightened sense of festivity. Their moral earnestness, though welcome, can make them too grim. Their burning desire for a better future world can sometimes prevent them from savoring this present one. In certain festive and fanciful moments history allows us to taste in the present the first fruits of what we hope for in the future.

The flaw in the new militants is that in their passion to live in a more human world they sometimes fail to relish those first fruits that are present today. They lack a festive élan. Earnest, committed, even zealous, they often suffer from a fatal humorlessness. Their "no" is so much louder than their "yes" that they seem to skirt very close to the borders of nihilism. But revolution need not be nihilistic. As Albert Camus himself says in *The Rebel,* one of the central texts for the new militants, "History may perhaps have an end; but our task is not to terminate it but to create it . . . The procedure of beauty, which is to contest reality while endowing it with unity, is also the procedure of rebellion." [7]

The great attractiveness of Camus, and the momentous truth he has to teach all who fight for a new society is that the basic task is creative not destructive, that "rebellion" cannot exist without "a strange form of love," and that love is not just for the future but for the present in all its torpor and turpitude. Can we wholeheartedly strive for a radically different tomorrow while at the same time affirming what is wholesome and human about today? Can we live occasionally in the tomorrow which has not yet come? If we cannot then cynicism seems almost inevitable. For Camus, however, whose main concern was to understand and participate in the great metaphysical rebellion of this age, cynicism need not conquer. "Is it possible," he asked, "to reject injustice without ceasing to acclaim the nature of man and the beauty of the world?" His answer was "yes."

That simple "yes" is a vitally important syllable, especially at a time when some serious radicals believe it is enough just to say "no." To say no is certainly important. And there are times when there is nothing to say but no. But in saying yes, as Camus knew, "we prepare the way for the day of regeneration." In saying "yes" along with our "no" we define the world we want "in the face of the world that insults it."

In a world as tortured by war and hunger as ours is, anything less than anger and resentment from the young would hardly seem reasonable. We do need a worldwide human revolution. In all of this the new militants are right. But as the history of revolutions so cruelly shows, today's zealous rebel can quickly become tomorrow's repressive tyrant. The revolution we need now must be more encompassing than those of China, Russia, or Cuba. We cannot derive revolutionary models from the past. We must create our own. What we can learn from the past is that rebellion, when it does not include "a strange form of love," fails.

The new militants have already derived in part from biblical faith a hunger and thirst for righteousness that makes the churches' concern for the Kingdom of God seem pale and irresolute. Yet in its secularized form, this passion runs the danger of collapsing into mere negation or noisy, ineffectual clamor. What Christianity, perhaps with the help of the neomystics, may bring to the new militants is a sense of festivity. Without for a moment tempering their ardor for a new tomorrow, one could help them to see, again in the words of Camus, that "real generosity toward the future lies in giving all to the present." If we can celebrate what we now are and have, even while we struggle to abolish the "now" for a better "not yet," the not yet will be richer when it becomes the now.

The neomystics are the "Catholics" of today's youth culture, and the new militants are the "Protestants." But just as Catholics and Protestants need each other in the church, so do the celebrators of life today and the seekers of justice tomorrow need each other in the world. Celebration without politics becomes effete and empty. Politics without celebration becomes mean and small. The festive spirit knows how to toast the future, drink the wine, and break the cup. They all belong together.

Beyond Radical Theology

8

How can the Christian faith exist and be real in a world and history in which God is dead? Radical theologians are united in their insistence that faith must exist fully in the actuality of our history, abandon all nostalgia for the lost world of Christendom, and seek the Christ who is real here and now for us.

—*Thomas J. J. Altizer,* Toward a New Christianity

The moment of truth has come for Christianity. It finds itself in a world that has nearly lost its capacity for either festivity or fantasy and is therefore close to extinction. That world is now beginning to reclaim these neglected dimensions of life, but it often does so in terms that seem antithetical to faith. Christianity seeks to keep man open to all the dimensions of time. Our present cultural renaissance, however, is almost obsessively preoccupied with the present and the future. Consequently Christianity often appears to be an obstacle to human renewal. It is frequently viewed as a relic of the past and an enemy of the spirit.

The contradiction is a fatal one. Unless the present rebirth of feeling and perception eventually links man to the history of the species and to the whole global village, it will falter and fail. Christianity could help add these needed dimensions. But unless Christianity frees itself from its preoccupation with the past, it cannot even make contact with the formative forces of modern culture. Can theology enable Christianity to overcome this mortal weakness so that it in turn can help nourish the renewal of our civilization?

Two current movements in theology give us hope that it may. They are, first, the largely American-based movement called "radical theology," and, second, the more European-based movement called "the theology of hope." Both of these movements bring encouragement to what has otherwise been a rather bleak theological situation. But, even taken together, they do not go far enough. If theology is to strengthen Christianity so it can make its contribution to the culture, it will need to absorb the insights of these two movements and then to move beyond them to an even more inventive theological approach.

Radical Theology

Though the radical theology movement, with its sensational "God is dead" slogan, no longer commands the headlines, its contribution to the renewal of faith and culture remains a significant one. Even those who opposed it during its zenith now admit that it was a welcome elixir. The radical movement frightened, challenged, and refreshed theology enormously. It did so in part precisely because of its willingness to deal with past traditions in a very unconventional way. T. J. J. Altizer, one of its best-known advocates, calls its approach "the method of creative negation." He says that theology will be able to enter our new world "only by effecting a *radical break* with its own past and by passing through a *dissolution* of its inherited form and language." [1] Let us sever the umbilical cord to the past, he says, adding that "the death of the theological tradition is at bottom its rebirth into new life." Thus radical theology joins the culture's immolation of the past. So far both Artaud and Cage would probably agree.

Why is this break needed? The answer advanced by the radicals is instructive. They say that a "decisive transformation of faith" has *already* occurred in the modern world and that this change must now be recognized by theology. The death-of-God theologian wants to look today's godless world unblinkingly in the face, to "abandon all nostalgia for the lost world of

Christendom." He does so, like some of the neomystics, by adopting a radically incarnational posture. He seeks, as Altizer says, "that Christ who is real here and now for us." [2] Here it begins to come clear that the radical theologian's interest in escaping from the past is essentially "Cageian" rather than "Artaudian." He wants to cut the cord to the past so that we can really live in the present. He insists that "faith must exist fully in the actuality of our history." Since the contemporary sensibility is, he claims, one of "radical immanence," a transcendent God is no longer real. The urgent theological question becomes "How can the Christian faith exist and be real in a world where God is dead?"

The major contribution of the radical movement and one reason why it has struck such a responsive chord with so many people is that it is not afraid to take our *present* spiritual experience earnestly *even when it so obviously contravenes the Christian tradition*. Radical theology, whatever its weaknesses, is not a victim of the compulsive quest for continuity. It has turned theology's attention once more to something that has fascinated such disparate figures as Friedrich Schleiermacher, William James, Douglas Clyde MacIntosh, and Abraham Maslow—namely, man's present experience of the holy.

But does radical theology take our present situation a bit too seriously? Despite William Hamilton's erstwhile talk of a "new optimism," most of radical theology is pervaded by a gloomy earnestness. Perhaps it should be. After all, as the Jewish death-of-God theologian Richard Rubenstein says, there is something undeniably sad about death, especially when it is the death of God. Radical theologians want to take the present religious mood seriously. Their key words are "the Christ in the here and now," "immanence," and "present actuality." But in its Cageian fascination with the sound of the soul today radical theology makes two mistakes. First, it overlooks the fact that Christ can be a shifty trickster who is sometimes neither here nor now. Second, it somehow misses the reemergence in the life of faith today of that mirthful and festive mood for which a mourning band is an inappropriate greeting.

In its insistence that faith must exist fully in the actuality of our present history, radical theology forgets that our present history is sometimes a paltry one and that in any case it represents only a portion of the reality open to a creature who also remembers, hopes, and imagines. Faith does not exist fully "within" any given situation. By its very nature faith breaks open the constrictiveness of the situation and points beyond it.

Today the theologian, like the novelist or any other artist, must cope with what Frank Kermode calls the clash between "an inherited paradigm" and "a changed sense of reality." [3] Radical theology deals with this clash simply by affirming one side, our changed sense of reality. It just disposes of the inherited paradigm. It thus represents an apotheosis of the present. But it somehow overlooks what Artaud knew—that the present is also a captor.

The death-of-God theology unlocks us from the prison of the past, but the escape route it provides leads to the dungeon of today. God is dead, but the present is divine. Wherever memory defies the sovereign will of the present, it is sacrificed, wherever tradition doesn't fit in it must go. It is held that this very act of negating the past gives the present its authenticity. Man becomes man by burning his bridges behind him. Radical theology is another instance of the ritual immolation of history.

And despite its attempt to be in touch with the mood of the moment, radical theology misses some very important aspects of that mood. Present experience is not a closed box. It opens out into the remembrance of things past and the "substance of things hoped for." Radical theology in its preoccupation with extricating the present from the past forgets that man's distinctive creativity springs from his capacity to reach out for what Ernst Bloch calls the "not yet." [4] Fantasy is an integral part of experience and an invaluable source of human freedom.

It expresses itself in man's freedom to see things which are *not*. In relying so exclusively on present experience radical theology leaves insufficient room for fantasy. By its total dependency on the here and now, it sacrifices what is *not* in the interest of what *is,* thus losing a critical point of leverage without which the present can become just as tyrannical as the past.

The death-of-God movement wants to interpret the life of faith, but it misses somehow the mood of festivity and playfulness in that life today. Its mood is sombre. It cannot cope with the exhilaration of an erotic underground movie or a guerilla theatre confrontation, or the raucous gaiety of a folk-rock festival or a jazz liturgy. In its absorption in "that Christ who is real here and now for us," it in fact misreads an important dimension of the very contemporary sensibility it strives to reach. Neither in the black urban revolt nor among the young political activists nor on frontiers of artistic creation today does one find such total deference for the here and now. All enjoy the now but are also actively focused on a "not yet" that our present social institutions and civilizational consciousness have so far failed to attain. Our mood today is a radical denial of the adequacy of the present. While enjoying to the utmost the present moment, we are also witnessing a spirited attack on what *is*. This sensibility can be witnessed in contemporary painting, cinema, and literature. Where it is most articulate, it ruthlessly assaults our present ways of thinking and behaving. It seeks to blow our minds and to smash the "here and now" into fragments, believing that in his way it can squeeze and shock us into a wholly new perception. It has Artaudian elements as well as Cageian. It proceeds on the premise that the present is not only incomplete but constrictive and distorted, that its modes of experience, far from providing the base line to which all else must be adjusted, are themselves rigid and eviscerating.

Not all radical theology canonizes the present. But insofar as it does it seriously misjudges our cultural mood. Though we hear talk of a "now generation," what we see is a sometimes nearly frantic dissatisfaction with the now and a search for what is new, untried, novel. It may have been accurate to label the contemporary sensibility "immanentist" a few years back. It is certainly no longer accurate in a period of op art, theatre of cruelty, astrology, electronic nonmusic, and multimedia cinema. Mere incarnational theology is no match for the aquarian age or the apocalyptic sensibility. Like John Cage and the neomystics, radical theology is a form of presentism. We can accept it as a symptom of our sickness, not as a solution. There is, however, another virile challenge to theology's preoccupation with the past—the contemporary movement known as the "theology of hope."

Theology of Hope

Associated with such men as Jürgen Moltmann, Gerhard Sauter, and Johannes Metz, the "theology of hope" is the most interesting theological movement to emerge from Europe since the demise of Barthianism, Bultmann's "demythologizing," and the endless arguments between exponents of these two schools. The new movement has two sources of inspiration. One is the scholarly interest in "eschatology" or the theology of the future which has preoccupied religious thinkers off and on for centuries, but has received special attention in our own century. The other source is our period's unusual interest in the future —in planning, projecting, and extrapolation, or in revolution— and the concern of theologians to communicate with people who do this sort of thinking. It is not surprising that the theologians of hope are among the main participants in the Christian-Marxist dialogue.

It came as a terrible shock to many Christians when theologians at the end of the nineteenth century discovered that Jesus was not a gentle teacher or exemplary social reformer but a man who really expected the end of the world to come in his time. This discovery, mainly the work of Johannes Weiss and Albert Schweitzer, punctured the popular image of Jesus and pushed Christianity into a debate that is still going on today. The question it posed is a prickly one: if Jesus' faith anticipated the imminent coming of a new age which in 1900 years has still not appeared, what possible validity does it have today?

Many different answers have been given to this question. Some theologians such as C. H. Dodd answered it by emphasizing the "already." Calling it "realized eschatology" they taught that in Jesus the Kingdom had already come and needed only to be realized in its fullness. Others such as Bultmann tended to internalize the Kingdom of God and see it as the "presence of eternity" in time. Still others, of course, held to the conventional notion that the Kingdom began after a person's individual death.

Now, however, the theologians of hope want to restore to Christian faith its future-oriented, expectant stance. As Jürgen Moltmann says,

From first to last, and not merely in the epilogue, Christianity is eschatology, is hope, forward looking and forward moving, and therefore also revolutionizing and transforming the present. The eschatological is not one element of Christianity, but is the medium of Christian faith as such, the key in which everything in it is set, the glow that suffuses everything here in the dawn of an expected new day.[5]

Hope now becomes the axis around which all other Christian virtues must find their place.

The other stimulus for the emergence of the theology of hope was Christianity's discovery that in a world characterized by its interest in the future, theology was mainly interested in the past. Johannes Metz, the best known Roman Catholic among the theologians of hope, says that, unless we have become mere antiquarians, the only legitimate interest theology should have in the past is in how it can help us create a new future. He claims that man's attitude toward the world today is not contemplative but operative; that is, seeing life not as something imposed on him by the past but something to be shaped for the future.[6] In conversations with Marxists, Metz argues that Christianity should be seen as "the religion of the absolute future" and that it posits a world that is more radically open to human domination than a world moved by the inexorable logic of a Marxist dialectic.

Moltmann and Metz are joined in their movement by a number of other young West German theologians such as Gerhard Sauter and, in some respects, Wolfhart Pannenberg. Several of them hold that Christianity lost its future stance and revolutionary potential when, as Moltmann puts it, it "became an organization . . . under the auspices of the Roman state religion and persistently upheld the claims of that religion." [7] He believes this forced the revolutionary impulse of Christianity to emigrate into sects and eventually into secular revolutionary movements. Moltmann wants to reclaim this impulse for Christianity. If he were to carry through his program every item in the register of theology would be reconstructed in light of future hope. Instead of a supernatural entity, God would become the ground of future possibility, a reality for whom "futurity is the essence of his being." He is not a God over us or a God within us, but as Metz says "Gott vor uns." Christ becomes the one who introduces a new age whose full reality is yet to appear. Christ is more important for Moltmann as the "coming one" than as the "historical Jesus" of Schweitzer or the "Christ, here and now" of the radicals. Our knowledge of Christ, he says, is "anticipatory, provisional and fragmentary knowledge of his future, namely of what he will be." [8] Faith is not belief but hope. Instead of the medieval formula "credo ut intelligam" (I believe that I may know), Moltmann suggests our formula today should be "spero ut intelligam" (I hope that I may know). The Church becomes the "exodus people" forever leaving the present behind and pushing toward an unknown future. As Metz says the tension between Church and world is not spatial but temporal; the Church should be ahead of the world in its movement toward the Kingdom of God. The common goal of both Church and world should be "to transform in opposition and creative expectation the face of the world in the midst of which one believes, hopes, and loves" [9]—this calls for a radical search for new institutions so that instead of serving the things that *were,* they serve instead "the things that are to come."

What can we say of this new movement? My first comment is that it represents a welcome change, especially in view of the fact that it stems from Germany. In America, the notion that faith should impel us into world transforming action is not a particularly new one. As H. Richard Niebuhr demonstrated decades ago, the idea of a coming Kingdom has always been central in American theology, and in Whitehead and Weiman there are philosophical sources for a God who makes change and innovation possible. What the new hope theologians have done is to ground their thinking in more traditional theological categories.

It is also evident that the theology of hope stands in sharp contrast to radical theology. Although radical theology glorifies the present, there is in theology of hope no reverence for present experience. Quite the contrary. The issue is, as Moltmann insists, "Does the present define the future through extrapolation or does the future define the present in anticipation?" [10] For Moltmann the answer is clear—the future defines the present. He also insists, again in vivid contrast to the American radicals, that the New Testament really knows of no Christ who is present for us in the "here and now." Christ is always present at the disappearing point where the future impinges on the present and is therefore never fully here or now. Further, Moltmann believes that the whole idea of a here and now as a kind of molecule of eternity is mistaken. The here and now, he insists, is always the starting point of a new and altered future.

It is almost too obvious to point out that the theology of hope exhibits a certain one-sidedness. Radical theology's mistake was to elevate *present* experience to divine status; the theology of hope comes perilously close to identifying God with the *future*. If radical theology falls prey to Cage's presentism, the theology of hope has some of the same dangers as Artaud's futurism. In order to agree that God is "before us" *must* we also say there is no "God within?" In analyzing the doxological formula about the God who "was and is and is to come," Moltmann puts enormous emphasis on the "is to come." He suggests that "is to come" differs from "shall be" in seeing the future as dynamic and open rather than as a mere continuation of the *is*. What he neglects to say, however, is that the doxological formula does say God was and *is*. Like some of the new political radicals, the theologians of hope fail to savor the present. They do not help us to hold together the three dimensions of temporality without collapsing one into another. How can this be done?

The answer to this question must be discussed on two levels. In the life of faith itself it comes with the reemergence in our time of a spirit of festivity and fantasy in religion. This revived sensibility frees man not to fear the past but to sing and dance about it as part of his own story. It enables him to visualize the future as an undiscovered country swarming with terrors and delights, luring him to fantasy.

At another level, however, the problem of our sense of discontinuity with our religious past and our tendency to overcompensate by exalting present experience or future hope requires a more subtle theological method. This book is mainly concerned with the life of faith, not with theological method. Still, some hints about the possible outline of such a method might be in order. This is especially true in view of the fact that it is the emergent sensibility in religious life that makes such a theological method possible.

A Theology of Juxtaposition

. . . juxtapose . . . contrast, oppose, set in opposition, set off against, put or set over against, place against, set over against one another, set or pit against one another; measure, weigh, balance.

—*Roget's* International Thesaurus, *3 ed., s.v. Comparison*

What sort of theological approach will match the present rebirth of festivity and fantasy? What theological method will help solve the problem that arises from our ambivalent attitude toward history? How can theology itself contribute to the rebirth of celebration and imagination that is now occurring in religion?

The theological method we need today cannot be content to explain and interpret the past. Nor can it focus entirely on present experience or bind itself wholly to future hope. Most importantly, it cannot try to smooth over the obvious contradictions in these dimensions of faith and experience nor attempt to reduce or reconcile them to each other. Rather it will accept and even exemplify the differences among these dimensions by juxtaposing them to each other. Recalling one of the principal ingredients of festivity, let us call this theological method the "method of juxtaposition."

A method of juxtaposition in theology should begin with "radical theology" by recognizing that our present is one of discontinuity and *is* real, not simply transient. It should go even further than the radicals, however, by assuming that this experience of tension between past, present, and future is valuable, and not merely something to escape. It should assume that the contradiction we feel today between what is and what has been should not be overcome by finding some way to negate the tradition. The experience of discontinuity is also an authentic one. It is the very oddness, incredibility, and even at points weirdness of traditional faith that makes it interesting to us today. A religion must be to some degree "out of step" with the assumptions of the era or it becomes banal. Juxtaposition sees the disrelation between inherited symbol and present situation not as a lamentable conflict to be resolved but as a piquant cacophony to be preserved.

Juxtaposition celebrates the collision of symbol and situation as the occasion for new experience and unprecedented perception. It denies the radical theologian's apotheosis of present experience, not just in the name of memory but in the name of fantasy. Along with radical theology it discards any nostalgia for the past, but in line with the theology of hope it admits to a nostalgia for the new. It therefore refuses to trim the symbol to fit the situation because it sees that, precisely in the bizarre conjoining of the two, both symbol and situation break open to disclose newer and richer perceptions of reality. It sees the friction between what was and what is providing the fuel for motion toward the not yet.

In his influential essay on the "Priest and the Jester," the Polish philosopher Leszek Kolakowski, although he is discussing philosophy, unwittingly provides us with a description of two approaches to theology, that of the priest and that of the jester. The priest, Kolakowski says, upholds "the cult of the final and the obvious contained in tradition," the jester's task is to "question what appears to be self-evident."

The philosophy of the jester is a philosophy which in every epoch denounces as doubtful what appears as unshakable; it points out the contradictions in what seems evident and incontestable; it ridicules common sense into the absurd—in other words, it undertakes the daily toil of the jester's profession along with the inevitable risk of appearing ludicrous.[1]

The juxtapositional approach is a method for theological jesters. It questions not only the self-evidence of the tradition but also the self-evidence of experience. It challenges the past from the perspective of present experience, and it challenges the present from the perspective of our memory of the past. It limits the claims of both past and present by thinking in light of hope. It is an instance of the "things which are *not* bringing to nought the things which are."

Let us risk what might be an instructive oversimplification. Traditional theologies emphasize faith's dependence on the past; they are historical. Radical theology, the "theology of creative negation," focuses on the present crisis of faith; it is incarnational. Theology of hope is oriented toward the future; it is eschatological. A theology of juxtaposition plays off the tensions among these three not by neatly balancing them but by maximizing the creative friction among all three. So it focuses precisely on those discomfiting points where memory, hope, and experience contradict and challenge each other. It recognizes our estrangement from much of the tradition, but it is also somewhat estranged from the ethos of today. It is unwilling to reconcile itself to either. It delights in the disrelation.

Conscious discontinuity with the tradition does not mean we either betray it or abandon it. Rather we use the tradition as the assumption from which a new departure is orbited. Calculated discontinuity exploits the friction between the past and the present to generate new possibilities for the future.

One of the best recent studies of the role of creative discontinuity is Morse Peckham's book *Man's Rage for Chaos*. Mr. Peckham, who as a student of aesthetics is just as uncomfortable with the state of his calling as many of us are with theology, starts off on a similar vein: "There is something seriously wrong," he says, "with the current and dominant conception of art. I believe that that serious wrongness lies exactly in the ancient effort to find order in a situation which offers us the opportunity to experience disorder. After so many centuries of praising order, I think it is time to praise disorder a little." [2] For the purposes of theology I would reword Mr. Peckham's paragraph slightly as follows: Our difficulty lies exactly in the ancient effort to establish continuity in a situation that offers us the opportunity to experience discontinuity. After so many centuries of praising continuity, it may be time to praise discontinuity a little.

But man is the creature who creates societies, builds cultures, and in many other ways seems to strive for order. Why should he seek experiences of disorder? Whence his rage for chaos? Peckham contends that the experience of art is "rehearsal experience." It helps us to live through those life experiences in which our orientation to the world is threatened by a reality that does not wholly comport with it.

In theological terms, man tries to be God. He finds himself in a changing unstable world but tries to arrange and order it so that he himself will not have to change. He does not want to live as a nomadic pilgrim. He wants the security of a closed system. But, "here we have no enduring city." God comes to man as the disturber of his peace, the one who will not allow him to settle down. The religious experience, like the aesthetic, is on one level an experience of disorder; but it points to another order, a city to come, which, though it is never fully attained, prevents man from being completely content with the present.

In theology the Christian redefinition of the messianic hope of Israel provides an excellent example of creative discontinuity. Without the expectations of Israel, Christian messianism would be meaningless. But Christian messianism did not fulfill Israel's expectations. It at once disappointed them and at the same time broadened and deepened them. Eschatology almost always has this jarring, juxtaposing function. It uses the tradition against itself. It recalls the fondly awaited day of the Lord but gives that day a different content: "It will be darkness, not light." It shatters traditional hopes by disclosing new and more sweeping promises. It utilizes the symbols and images of the tradition to "blow people's minds" and crack open traditional institutions. Perhaps our contemporary revival of eschatology will tear away our timid, measly hopes and restore a really radical vision. It will do so, however, only if it focuses not on the *content* of traditional religious hopes but on the radicalizing *form* of their relation to the tradition and the impact they had on consciousness.

Juxtaposition has other links with the theology of hope. Moltmann has argued that the task of theology is not to reconcile faith to experience but to introduce a note of creative conflict, which juxtaposition does. He has also stated, taking a leaf from the notebook of Karl Marx, that theology has interpreted experience for long enough, that the thing to do now is to *change* it. This suggests that the task of theologians is not to come to terms with existing patterns of perception but to explode them, not merely to speak to existing social structures but to undermine them. Merely to reconcile theology to existing reality is to forget the crucial eschatological factor, the one that reminds us that existing reality is provisional, is part of "this passing age," and therefore cannot be taken with ultimate seriousness.

Perhaps the artistic movement that comes closest to this juxtapositional theology is surrealism. In painting surrealism has been associated with the names of Magritte, Ernst, Dali, Chirico, and others. But as Susan Sontag has pointed out in her essay on happenings, surrealism is "a mode of sensibility which cuts across all the arts in the 20th century," including poetry, cinema, music, and even architecture.[3] "The Surrealist tradition in all these arts," Miss Sontag continues, "is united by the idea of destroying conventional meanings, and creating new meanings or counter-meanings through radical juxtaposition (the 'collage principle')." Surrealism stresses the extremes of disrelation, which is the subject of comedy, rather than relatedness, which is the subject of tragedy.

Again it should be emphasized that surrealism does not abandon or discard the artistic tradition. Art began in human society as a magical and religious activity. It later became a technique for commenting on social reality. Today, Miss Sontag observes, art has become "an instrument for modifying consciousness and organizing new modes of sensibility." Art is not merely a vehicle for ideas. It is rather an instrument for modifying consciousness, for "changing the composition . . . of the humus that nourishes all specific ideas and sentiments." At issue here seems to be an insight shared by both Marxists and McLuhanites, that changes in the technology and organization of society tend to anesthetize us, to dim our awareness. What we need is a newly awakened perception of what is now going on and a vision of what could. This is the aim of a theology of juxtaposition.

Can a theology of juxtaposition move us away from our present theological impasse? If the sensibility epitomized by various forms of surrealism has any validity, we will break through to a new theological style not by papering over the difficulties but precisely by stressing the disrelation we feel between us and what has gone before. If Kolakowski is right that this is basically a jester's method, it does not mean the situation is simply funny. Although the jester does often make us laugh, his function is to sharpen our critical awareness. He mocks and ridicules the very things we are most reticent to reexamine.

It might be objected that whereas the task of reconciling the tradition to the present, the classical theological enterprise, is a difficult one, juxtaposition is the lazy man's way out. Nothing could be further from the truth. Real juxtaposition is not random mishmash. It requires the most skillful and imaginative work. It demands both a firm grasp of the tradition, and an insight into modern sensibility, plus a capacity to juxtapose them in a way that will introduce a new critical awareness, and a fresh appreciation for both.

No doubt there are dangers in a juxtapositional theology just as there are in any comic style. When tragedy fails you still have pathos. When comedy fails it becomes ridiculous. When tragedy succeeds it reveals to us a vision of the relentless wholeness of life. When comedy succeeds it shakes us into a new stance, it prepares us for new experiences. Yet one could argue that the great breakthroughs in the history of theology have always introduced notes of cacophony and dissonance. They have been discontinuous (heretical) from the perspective of their immediate contemporaries. Only in retrospect do we trace out the continuity and include them in the unfolding drama of development.

But even if a theology of juxtaposition might help us, is there any chance that we can develop one? Ways of thinking are always linked to particular patterns of social relations. A new intellectual approach in theology will require a different social location for the theologian. You cannot expect jester's theology from the archbishop's palace. Nor can a church that merely sanctifies society or pursues "relevance" at all costs produce any refreshing juxtapositions. How can the church kick off the remains of its velvet Constantinian trap and assume a more comical and critical relation to society?

Here again the metaphor of the jester may help. Kolakowski describes the jester's relationship to society this way:

Although an habitué of good society, [he] does not belong to it and makes it the object of his inquisitive impertinence; he . . . questions what appears to be self-evident. The jester could not do this if he himself were part of the good society, for then he would be, at the most, a drawing room wit. A jester must remain an outsider; he must observe "good society" from the sidelines, for only then can he detect the non-obvious behind the obvious and the non-final behind what appears to be final.

At the same time he must frequent good society so as to know what it deems holy, and to be able to indulge in his impertinence.[4]

To "frequent" good society but not to belong to it; to be its "habitué" and at the same time to observe it from the sidelines —this sounds very much like St. Paul's suggestion that the church should be "in but not of the world."

I believe this means for our time a reappropriation of the radical utopian, sectarian and monastic impulses in Christianity. It means a rediscovery of styles of Christian life and images of Christ that in recent years have nearly been forgotten. But here again, the life of the spirit is ahead of the theologians. The modern equivalent of monastic communities have already begun to appear in today's communes and co-ops. And the image of Christ as the jester has begun to appear too.

Christic the Harlequin 10

For the foolishness of God is wiser than men, and the weakness of God is stronger than men.

—*St. Paul,* First Epistle to the Corinthians

Christ has come to previous generations in various guises, as teacher, as judge, as healer. In today's world these traditional images of Christ have lost much of their power. Now in a new, or really an old but recaptured guise, Christ has made an unexpected entrance onto the stage of modern secular life. Enter Christ the harlequin: the personification of festivity and fantasy in an age that had almost lost both. Coming now in greasepaint and halo, this Christ is able to touch our jaded modern consciousness as other images of Christ cannot.

The representation of Christ as a clown is still scattered and spotty. The artist Georges Rouault, drawing on his profound feel both for the microcosm of the circus and the French Catholic tradition, was perhaps the first person in modern times to make the identification explicit. But there were hints before him, and since his time the theme has become more widespread. One of the clearest instances occurred in the movie *The Parable,* produced for the Protestant pavilion at the 1966 New York World's Fair. In that film, although the Christ figure remained entirely too remote and ethereal, still his appearing as a circus clown touched and annoyed people in ways that more traditional depictions would certainly have failed to do.

Presenting Christ in the cap and spots of the clown could not have happened, of course, were it not for the striking reemergence of the clown in the contemporary secular imagination. Our era is blessed with a wealth of various and talented clowns: Charlie Chaplin, Buster Keaton, and the Marx Brothers. Though these inspired mimes went into partial eclipse at one point, film festivals constantly bring them to view again, and a whole new generation is discovering their charms. We also have Picasso's languid harlequins and the Rilke poem they inspired. We have the magicians and acrobats who appear in almost all the films of Federico Fellini. We have America's new breed of satirical comedians. We have Genêt's minstrel play, *The Blacks,* and Beckett's traditional carnival vagabonds in- *Waiting for Godot.* Recently the City Center Joffrey Ballet presented a parabolic ballet by Gerald Arpino entitled *The Clowns.* In it, clowns personify the hope for rebirth in a dying civilization. In literature, we have Oscar Mazerath in Günter Grass's *The Tin Drum,*[1] and a score of picaresque heroes in other recent novels. Maybe even the Beatles should be counted in. In any case, clowns and troubadors are back tumbling and frisking through our cultural imagination. They help set the stage for a new iconography of Christ.

Not really so new at that, since the symbol of Christ as clown has deep historical roots. One of the earliest representations of Christ in Christian art depicts a crucified human figure with the head of an ass. For years experts have disputed about what it means. Some think it may be an arcane sign, others a cruel parody. Either could be the case. But it might also be true that those catacomb Christians had a deeper sense of the comic absurdity of their position than we think they did. A wretched band of slaves, derelicts, and square pegs, they must have sensed occasionally how ludicrous their claims appeared. They knew they were "fools for Christ," but also claimed that the foolishness of God is wiser than the wisdom of men. Christ himself for them must have been something of a holy fool.

Furthermore, even in the biblical portrait of Christ there are elements that can easily suggest clown symbols. Like the jester, Christ defies custom and scorns crowned heads. Like a wandering troubador he has no place to lay his head. Like the clown in the circus parade, he satirizes existing authority by riding into town replete with regal pageantry when he has no earthly power. Like a minstrel he frequents dinners and parties. At the end he is costumed by his enemies in a mocking caricature of royal paraphernalia. He is crucified amidst sniggers and taunts with a sign over his head that lampoons his laughable claim.

The symbol of Christ the clown seems imminently right for the earliest period of Christian history. It could not persist, however, when the church's view of itself moved from the ridiculous to the sublime. What place is there for caricature when the church's regal vestments are taken seriously? When its crowns and sceptres are made of real gold instead of thorns and wood? A church that actually holds power and reigns has little capacity for self-caricature or irony. So during most of the centuries of Christendom, with an exception here and there, the image of Christ the clown disappeared, at least officially. The carnival spirit persisted in the medieval street skits and morality plays. Though the hierarchy often disapproved, the comic gait, with its suggestion of ambivalence and self-parody never completely disappeared. It simply went underground. Only now, in our secularized, postChristian era, is it able to emerge again. A weak, even ridiculous church, somehow peculiarly at odds with the ruling assumptions of its day, can once again appreciate the harlequinesque Christ. His pathos, his weakness, his irony—all begin to make a strange kind of sense again.

But why a clown Christ in a century of tension and terror? The clown represents different things to different people. For some he is the handy butt of our own fears and insecurities. We can jeer at his clumsy failures because they did not happen to us. For some he shows what an absurd clod man really is, and he allows us on occasion to admit it. For others he reveals to us our stubborn human unwillingness to be encaged forever within the boundaries of physical laws and social proprieties.

The clown is constantly defeated, tricked, humiliated, and tromped upon. He is infinitely vulnerable, but never finally defeated.

In representing Christ as a clown our generation probably senses, at least intuitively, that the painted grin and motley suit carry all these multiple meanings, and more. The very ambiguity of the cap and bells somehow suits our wistful, ironic attitude toward Christ. To Christ's pointed question of Peter, "Who do you say that I am?" we can no longer conscientiously spout the conventional replies. So we clothe Christ in a clownsuit, and that way we express many things at once: our doubts, our disillusionment, our fascination, our ironic hope.

But we say something else too, something more distinctively contemporary. We say that our whole relation to Christ, to any faith at all, and to the whole of existence for that matter, is one of conscious play and comic equivocation. Only by assuming a playful attitude toward our religious tradition can we possibly make any sense of it. Only by learning to laugh at the hopelessness around us can we touch the hem of hope. Christ the clown signifies our playful appreciation of the past and our comic refusal to accept the spectre of inevitability in the future. He is the incarnation of festivity and fantasy.

Faith as Play

In the form and function of play, itself an independent entity which is senseless and irrational, man's consciousness that he is embedded in a sacred order of things finds its first, highest, and holiest expression.

Johan Huizinga, Homo Ludens

With Christ the harlequin, even the churches seem once again to be learning how to play. Dance, lights, rollicking music, mime, and ritual feasting are making their appearance again in the chilly, grey sanctuaries of Christianity. True, they had never really disappeared from Black Protestantism, Mediterranean Catholicism or from Hasidic Judaism. But their recent general return is part of the festivity Christ embodies.

A good example of this playful esprit in the church is the art of Sister Corita Kent. Sister Corita's approach is tongue in cheek. She drolly steals slogans from our all-encompassing mass-media environment and splatters them helter skelter on bright paper set off by gay colors and shapes. A Christmas poster peals, "He cared enough to send the very best." Easter's message is "Come alive!"

This sardonic juxtaposition at once makes fun of the advertiser's messages and also squeezes out of them a significance they never intended. This much is noticeable immediately. But the breezy messages also may say something else. They enable us to restate classical Christian themes in a sportive style. This way we can affirm them without doing it in the traditional solemn way. In using our society's icons to say something different in an ironical manner, we heap nuance upon nuance and combine satire, hope, and playfulness.

Sister Corita's art of the prankster is analogous to the theology of the jester. The impact on the viewer is similar. Both assemble elements that appear to be incongruent, but in both the resulting collage is a frisky caper with a serious intent: we are made to see things in a new way.

Whether consciously or not, the rompish style of Sister Corita's art depends on a profound truth about man—his capacity to hold two or more seemingly contradictory ideas or emotions at once. This strange human capacity is not something our age has discovered. It has been noticed by acute observers of the human heart for ages. Men are able at one and the same time to laugh, worship, fear, be fascinated, be curious and repulsed, and even to love and hate. But different ages seem to develop this capacity in different directions. Succeeding epochs have their own set of seemingly contradictory postures to balance and reconcile.

For us today the problem is how to reconcile a high degree of critical self-consciousness with a burning desire for experience, which is not spoiled by too much self-analysis. The popularization of social science has made us all painfully aware of the sources of our feelings and ideas. Yet we also yearn for joyful immediacy. We want to believe but we are unable. We want to be coolly sophisticated yet not lose the simple directness we think is vital in human life. Is such a posture possible?

Christ the harlequin, the man of sorrows in the foolscap, symbolizes just this combination of merriment and seriousness. Henri Bergson in his famous essay on laughter said that a situation is invariably comic if it belongs simultaneously to two independent series of events and is capable of being interpreted in two entirely different meanings at the same time.[2] This is the sensibility that is played out so well in Sister Corita's art. It is a sensibility that both makes the harlequin Christ possible, and in turn is enriched by his mimicry. The problem is this: as sophisticated and self-critical postmoderns we know our religious symbols are human phenomena. We are often bored with them. We know our beliefs are historically conditioned and our faith influenced by social factors galore. We are no longer even interested in doubting them. The coming of Christ the harlequin means, however, that symbols, belief, and faith need not simply be jettisoned. That was the simple-minded critical response of an earlier generation, one that had not yet uncovered for itself the playful element even in such a serious thing as faith. Our ability to laugh while praying is an invaluable gift. It is not understood either by the sober believers or by the even more sober atheists among us.

In late 1967 Maurice Bejart's *Mass for the Present Time* was wildly acclaimed at the Théatre National Populaire in Paris. The *Mass* included the recitation of a passage from Nietzsche's *Thus Spake Zarathustra,* a black-clad witch racing around the stage on a motor scooter, rock music, electronic chords, the roar of jet engines, and a reading from Song of Songs. The whole thing sounds bizarre, and probably was. But Bejart himself uses the word "liturgy" for what he was doing. He described it as "a joke in the middle of a prayer. If you can joke about something very important," he said, "you have achieved freedom." [3]

Christ the harlequin is the joke in the middle of the prayer. Even better, perhaps, he is the prayer as joke or the joke as prayer. He is the spirit of play in a world of calculated utilitarian seriousness. It is a spirit for which Christianity ironically enough has somehow become one of the few remaining spokesmen and guardians. In the United States, a land of puritan Protestantism and jansenist Catholicism, this comes as a surprise. But it should not be as surprising as all that. The close kinship of play and religion is something scholars have been uncovering for some years now.

Johan Huizinga has discussed the relationship between religion and play in his book *Homo Ludens*.[4] He points out that ritual and religion actually emerged very long ago in man's capacity for play. In tribal societies ritual is obviously loaded with play acting and "make believe." The men carve the masks and then scare each other with them. The women, who know full well their husbands and brothers are behind the masks, scream in terror at them. In ritual cures a certain complicity of doctor and patient is obviously involved. In the hunt and fertility dances, the dancers "become" the animals and clouds, but they know full well they are enacting these parts.

Despite this evidence many people still have great difficulty in seeing religion as a form of play. The difficulty arises from two sources. First, they have been taught to place "play" at a very low level of importance. This, however, is the prejudice of an industrial society, and is in no sense a universal judgment. Plato in *The Laws* not only made worship a form of play but taught that "life must be lived as play." Second, many people believe one cannot be "serious" about play. These critics have obviously never watched a masters bridge tournament. Man *can* be very serious about play, and can take even the most serious things quite playfully.

But even in Christian theology the idea of liturgy as a form of play is not new. The point was made over forty years ago by the Roman Catholic scholar Romano Guardini who in his book *The Spirit of the Liturgy,* included a chapter entitled "Liturgy as Play." [5]

Still the idea of worship as play is not widely known or accepted in most places. Consequently, when in 1967 Sister Corita Kent published a book entitled *Footnotes and Headlines,* and subtitled *A Pray and Play Book,*[6] the fat was in the fire again. Many people were shocked. Praying and playing seemed after all to be such utterly disparate activities. Does not prayer require the complete exclusion of levity? Would not play, on the other hand, only be ruined by the sobriety and resolution of prayer?

The book joined the issue in a very clear way. What is the relation between prayer and play? The answer is a crucial one because on it depends the validity of the playful spirit in Christianity. Prayer is undeniably central to religious life. Thus, if prayer and play are inimical, or perhaps even mutually exclusive, then the prayer/play sensibility is dangerous and misleading for both. Christ the harlequin is an imposter. If, however, there is something profoundly similar about them, then our present reappropriation of the play element in Christianity is both welcome and appropriate.

In my view, not only are prayer and play analogous but their kinship provides us with a sound contemporary access both to our religious tradition and to the future.

In his book on *Man at Play,* the Roman Catholic philosopher Hugo Rahner describes *play* in words that could be used almost verbatim to describe *prayer.*

To play is to yield oneself to a kind of magic, to enact to one-
self the absolutely other, to pre-empt the future, to give the lie
to the inconvenient world of fact. In play earthly realities be-
come, of a sudden, things of the transient moment, presently
left behind, then disposed of and buried in the past; the mind
is prepared to accept the unimagined and incredible, to enter
a world where different laws apply, to be relieved of all the
weights that bear it down, to be free, kingly, unfettered and
divine.[7]

In light of this description of play it becomes clear that in
several ways prayer and play are strikingly similar. Both are
acts of disciplined fantasy. In both we "yield to a kind of
magic." Neither prayer nor play is limited or circumscribed by
the "inconvenient world of fact." Both go beyond it. How does
this apply to conventional forms of prayer? There are four
traditional forms of prayer: supplication, intercession, thanksgiving, and penitence. Each can be understood as a form of
play.

(1) In what are traditionally called prayers of *supplication,*
the person places himself in a still nonexistent future situation
that is richer, in some important respect, from his present. In
the fantasy of prayer he has obtained something he longs for
or he has rid himself of something he doesn't want. In theistic
traditions this prayer takes the form of asking God for something. In religions without a belief in such a god, it takes the
form of meditating on the condition to be achieved and mentally exploring ways to achieve it. In both, prayer, like play, is
an exercise in ordered imagination.

(2) In those prayers that are called *intercessory,* the praying person places himself in someone else's boots, usually someone who is "afflicted in mind, body, or estate." Prayer in this
instance involves a double level of fantasy. The praying person
must identify emotionally with the other person and must

imagine also a future in which his needs have been met. One of the earliest and most persistent forms of human play is pretending to be someone else. Intercessory prayer is a refinement deepened by love of this elementary kind of play.

(3) Play can also be gala and festive, just as one important form of prayer is *thanksgiving*. To express gratitude, bliss, or just plain joy we sing, dance, clap our hands, embrace each other. In Christianity this joy is directed toward the source of human felicity. But the addressee of the squeal of happiness is less important than its genuineness. All real prayers of thanksgiving, however inarticulate and to whomever addressed, are the whoops and hurrahs of a creature who is glad about something. As such, they are expressions of play: the elegant Prayer of General Thanksgiving, in *The Book of Common Prayer*, the raucous village fandango, the child jumping up and down as he opens a present.

(4) What about prayers of *penitence*, asking for forgiveness? Here, also the fantasy element becomes obvious with careful scrutiny. To pray for forgiveness is to see oneself in perspective and to strive consciously for a new role. It is to act "as if" one were not bound by the past and, in pretending, to be in fact freed from it. The objective side of the Christian notion of repentance is that the future is not just a continuation of the past. The unexpected and unprecedented can happen. Men are not fated by tragic flaws but free to start over. Penitence simply means starting out in a new direction. This is not possible in a world of inexorable necessity. It is possible in an open world of unlimited possibilities.

Prayer whether spoken, danced, or sung provides a form for human fantasy. By praying, a man shows that he is not a slave of the past, of the "facts" or of fate. When the structure of a prayer is provided by ritual themes and historical images the prayer is a bridge to the future. It produces action toward a goal. It is not an escape from the world but the first step in its recreation.

Religious leaders sometimes wring their hands today because they believe people do not pray as much as they used to. Prayer however is a much deeper and more pervasive part of human life than most books about it suggest. It includes far more than the narrow range of acts to which the word "prayer" has been attached in Christianity. Anyone who gives vent to joy, sorrow, or gratitude, or refuses to be bound by the narrow world of facts is really living a prayer. Faith too is more than mindless credulity. Both prayer and faith are really forms of play. Therefore it is pointless to lament the passing of a particular, dated style of prayer or the disappearance of a narrow notion of faith. Rather we should exult in the fact that a fascinating Man in a tessellated cap is teaching us how to play.

Christianity as Comedy

He thought he saw an Argument
* That proved he was the Pope:*
He looked again, and found it was
* A Bar of Mottled Soap.*
"A fact so dread," he faintly said,
* Extinguishes all hope!"*

—*Lewis Carroll, "The Mad Gardener's Song"*

For years theologians with a flair for literature have discussed Christianity in relation to the tragic. More recently, however, the tide has begun to turn and we have begun to see an increasing amount of work on Christianity and the comic sensibility. The comic, of course, has to do with more than the funny. It is a perspective on life.

But what perspective? Nathan Scott makes comedy a way of affirming creation, and Falstaff is the comic figure *par excellence*. In comedy, he says, we learn to see and love man, "warts and all." [8] Comedy disports in the mud and gumminess of life, It has no pretensions. It saves us from trying to be angels, and allows us to say with no apology, "I'm only human." Scott's is an incarnational view of the comic ingredient in Christianity.

Quite a different point of view is found in Peter Berger's theologico-social essay *The Precarious Vision*.[9] Here Berger sees eschatology as the comic element in Christianity. The clown refuses to live inside this present reality. He senses another one. He defies the law of gravity, taunts the policeman, ridicules the other performers. Through him we catch a glimpse of another world impinging on this one, upsetting its rules and practices.

Nelvin Vos, one of the most recent and articulate theological commentators on comedy, manages to combine elements of these perspectives by depicting Christ, following St. Augustine, as both victim and victor. We laugh both *at* and *with* the comic victor/victim because "he is the image of dignity intermingled with frailty." He both unmasks "the incongruous involvement of the finite with the infinite" and also affirms it. He helps us see "that the grossly human and the grandly sublime" are "wonderfully and repugnantly" mixed within us.

Both Scott and Berger, and most of the other theologians who have discussed the subject, agree, however, that the comic spirit is somehow closer to Christianity than is the tragic. In tragedy the hero first defies, then accepts, as he must, the inexorable. He is a fated man. His heroism emerges if he can meet his fate with dignity and manliness. The comic figure may be neither dignified nor manly. Few of us are. But he reveals the clay feet of the monolith. He makes us glad. In tragedy we weep and are purged. In comedy we laugh and hope.

It is strange in a way that Christian theology lost sight for so many years of the comic sensibility. Dante, perhaps the greatest Christian poet of any era, did, after all, name his masterpiece *The Divine Comedy*. Don Quixote, the creation of Cervantes' consummate Catholic imagination, is certainly a comic figure in the largest sense of the term. At the time these men wrote, sculptors were carving gargoyles on cathedrals and artists were painting pictures of an infant God sitting in his mother's arms playing with the globe of the earth. *Deus Ludens* is the playing God. He winks at man, his all-too-serious creature, disclosing to him the comic dimensions of it all. Yet these artists and writers were not theologians. What about the formal theological thinkers themselves?

It is true that at least one medieval theologian, Petrus Cantor, is known to have asked during the course of his ruminations whether Christ ever laughed. Cantor was of the solemn opinion that he must have if he was truly man. What disturbs us today is that Cantor should ever have felt the need to ask the question. Other theologians did a little better, but not much.

The Greek fathers contended that the creation of the world was a form of play. God did it they insisted out of freedom, not because he had to, spontaneously and not in obedience to some inexorable law of necessity. He did it, so to speak, "just for the hell of it." Some of these theologians also argued that the eternal logos, later to be incarnated in the son, was there within the father at creation to celebrate it and to give the father joy in the creation. Hugo Rahner, a contemporary Roman Catholic thinker, agrees. He believes that the Hebrew word in the book of Proverbs which describes the activity of the Logos can better be described as "dance." It is the same word used in II Samuel 6:5 and 6:21 to describe David's notorious dance before the ark of the Lord.[10]

Though the interpretation may be questionable, the thought is a scintillating one. Long before he lay powerless in the manger, drove the racketeers from the temple or hung on the cross, the spirit of Christ was present at the creation—dancing. This might have provided exegetes and theologians with one basis for discussing the comic.

But it did not. Despite the hints, the basic theological work on comedy has been done only quite recently. Most of it can be summed up in the notion that both for Christianity and for the comic sensibility nothing in life should be taken too seriously. The world is important but not ultimately so. Like the clown, the man of faith can snicker at the pretence of the prince because he knows the prince is but a man who will return one day to the dust. But more than that, the man of faith can even chuckle at his own snickering. He can see the prince and himself in a perspective that cuts both down to size but also opens to both new worlds of possibility.

The comic is rooted in faith. As one writer puts it: "The inner essence of humour lies, no matter how heretical this may seem, in the strength of the religious disposition; for what humour does is to note how far all earthly and human things fall short of the measure of God." [11] This growing consensus about the comic orientation of Christianity is another reason for the reemergence of Christ the clown.

True, there have been objections to the notion that Christianity gives rise to a comic sensibility. The objections come at three levels. The first claims to be biblical. It contends there is "nothing funny about the Bible," and thus asserts that the comic is foreign to Christianity. This criticism fails, however, because the Bible does have its comic side. God himself "laughs at the wicked" the Psalmist says, because he foresees their downfall. Noah, like Jonah, is pictured as an inept buffoon. Morality plays for centuries correctly played him with slapstick and pratfall. His wife was always a loquacious hussy. When the senile Sarah gives birth to a son, she names him "laughter" (Isaac) because having a child at her age was certainly a joke. There is satire in Isaiah's famous description of the oafish idol makers, ribaldry in the yarn about David and Bathsheba, and bawdy hyperbole in Elijah's tirades against the prophets of Baal on Mt. Carmel.

The New Testament, though somewhat less attuned to the comic, has its share of satire and grotesquerie. "Why," asks Lawrence Durrell in *Clea*, "don't they recognize in Jesus the great ironist that he is, the comedian?" [12] The comic sensibility is not foreign to the Bible.

A second level of criticism is theological. It holds that the comic is possible in other religious traditions but not in Christianity. The reason advanced is that since for some faiths the world is *maya,* a form of illusion, it need not be taken seriously. This makes possible the fascinating theme of "Lilia" or divine play in Hinduism. But because Christianity is grounded in historical events, so the argument runs, such comic detachment is not possible.

This argument is a more telling one but it also fails to withstand careful scrutiny. The point in Christianity is not that the world is "unreal" but that it should not be taken with ultimate or final seriousness. Thus the biblical form of humor tends to be satire or caricature. lending credence to Thornton Wilder's remark that "the comic tradition in the theatre carries the intention of exposing folly and curbing excess." [13] Thus Christianity does share a sense of comedy with other traditions. But its grounds are different. Instead of one world of shadow and deception it affirms two real world ages, the passing one and the coming one, neither of which should be seen without reference to the other, or taken with full seriousness on its own. We live "in between."

Finally, there is the ethical objection. Some sensitive people claim that laughter is not an appropriate response to war, racism, hunger, and injustice. Only serious dedication and sacrifice will ever rid the earth of these pestilences. They are right. But neither seriousness nor dedication, as we have shown before, is the opposite of the comic. The opposite of the comic is tragic necessity and perhaps even stoic resignation. The comic sensibility can laugh at those who ferment wars and perpetuate hunger, at the same time it struggles to dethrone them. It foresees their downfall even when their power seems secure. The comic, more than the tragic, because it ignites hope, leads to more, not less, participation in the struggle for a just world.

There is also, however, a vexing philosophical problem that lurks in the depths of the question of religion and the comic sensibility. It is the question of whether a human being can ever stand far enough back from his own religion (or irreligion) to get any "comic perspective." Religion or its equivalent provides our root orientation to reality. How do we "step back" from it without toppling into the abyss? Can we "step back" from the symbols of our own religion or would such a step merely indicate that these symbols are not really important for us, that there is another and larger system we are part of, one we might not be willing to laugh about?

This fascinating question has called forth two contradictory answers in recent philosophical history. One answer is represented by Hegel and Husserl. Both believed in their own way that a man *can* stand back from his own life symbols. Hegel relied on the power of the mind to see religious themes in the perspective of cultural history. Husserl depended on the method he called "bracketing," that is, scrutinizing a symbol or experience without asking about its final truth or validity.

The opposite answer is given by Kierkegaard and Heidegger. Neither believed that such a perspective is possible. For Kierkegaard one always has to be "inside" *some* order of existence. Though a person can have a sense of comic distance about someone else's ultimate symbols he cannot have such a perspective about his own. Otherwise he would not be existing at all. Heidegger makes something of the same point by arguing that symbols provide our *access* to reality. They make possible our perception, therefore we cannot look *at* them—we look *through* them.

The comic sensibility suggests a solution to this debate that affirms the truth on both sides. We are able to gain perspective, even on our most cherished beliefs and values. But we do so not by moving beyond symbol worlds, rather we do so by juxtaposing them. Bergson's theory that the comic occurs in a situation open to disparate orders of interpretation suggests that man is capable of living in these disparate spheres. Their very disparity supplies the leverage for the comic perspective. It is not only modern man with his multiple symbol worlds who stands astride this fulcrum. Primitive man had it too insofar as he recognized the curious discrepancy between the worlds of fact and fantasy. Wherever men live at the vortex of multiple worlds of meaning, the comic is possible. Only in a closed, monolithic universe is it excluded. Such a sober universe can be created by an inquisitorial religion, by a totalitarian state, or by a sleekly efficient technocracy. In the first two, however, there remain resources for comic criticism as the bawdy street plays of the medieval period and the underground jokes in police states prove. In fact, it is the rulers' fear of heresy and dissent that produces the thumb screw and the gestapo. The horror of the technically ruled society is that no such tortures are even needed. Dissent is quashed in more subtle ways and comic criticism is killed by kindness. Certainly technological blandness is more our danger today than either clericalism or state terror. This may be why Wolfgang Zucker in a brilliant essay on the clown says that in a world tending toward "absolute mechanization" and faced with the "myth of an unchanging mechanism," the clown, once nearly lost to our consciousness, "becomes necessary again." He is the one who "affirms by denying." [14]

Zucker is right. The clown does affirm by denying. But in denying he is also affirming. He enables us to laugh at our failures and successes, at our fears and also our faith. By involving us in his denial he lures us into affirming after all.

If playfulness is the only way we can deal with our past, laughter enables us to live with the future. Laughter of course can be strained, cruel, artificial, or merely habitual. It can mask our true feelings. But where it is real, laughter is the voice of faith. It is the expression not only of our ironic confidence and our strange joy, but also of our recognition that there is no "factual" basis for either. Perhaps that is why Dante reports that when he finally arrived in Paradise after his arduous climb from the Inferno, he heard the choirs of angels singing praises to the Trinity and, he says, "mi sembiana un riso dell universo" (it seemed like the laughter of the universe).

The laughter of the universe in heaven? Of course. In hell there is no hope and no laughter, according to Dante. In purgatory there is no laughter, but there is hope. In heaven, hope is no longer necessary and laughter reigns.

Comic hope is the mood of our embryonic religious sensibility today. It has left behind orthodox credulity, existential pathos, and sanguine optimism. It supplies the only possible idiom for faith at a time of dead gods, museum churches, and antiquarian theology. The new theologians are right that hope is the characteristic form of faith for modern man. But our hope is neither the serene confidence of medieval man, nor the liberal's bright expectation of better things around the corner. Ours is a more or less formless hope, but a hope nonetheless. It is a hope in search of content, a hope that some form of hope will once again be made available to us.

Given the empirical evidence around us this hope can be held only in the most daring act of effrontery. We cope with such totally unfunny challenges as war, death, and gratituitous suffering today in a comic vein that would have repelled a previous generation and still shocks many today. Joseph Heller's zany novel *Catch-22*, though it outrages many who know from experience the ghastliness of war, still finds a way to damn the senselessness of the whole thing in comic hyperbole.[15] It tells the story of a victimized World War II bombing-plane captain named Yossarian who, though literally mad and quite paranoid by the end of the book, comes off as the only sane man in it. His cowardice and craziness seem, in contrast to the ponderous logic of the generals and colonels around him, the only rational course. *Catch-22* is not just about war. It is about the ultimate madness that lies at the base of our ever-so-rational society. It tries, as one critic says, to "reveal the essential fraudulence within the horror, to uncover the ridiculousness within the catastrophe; in the hope at least of letting in a little light." [16]

Laughter is hope's last weapon. Crowded on all sides with idiocy and ugliness, pushed to concede that the final apocalypse seems to be upon us, we seem nonetheless to nourish laughter as our only remaining defense. In the presence of disaster and death we laugh instead of crossing ourselves. Or perhaps better stated, our laughter is our way of crossing ourselves. It shows that despite the disappearance of any empirical basis for hope, we have not stopped hoping. As R. W. B. Lewis says, our sense of the awful nearness of catastrophe lies close to the heart of the imagination today. But it does not paralyze the heart itself. At the very heart of man there lies "a humane perspective rooted not quite in hope but in a hope about hope."

This sense of irrepressible radical hope remains alive and well, in the comic. Its Christ is the painted jester whose foolishness is wiser than wisdom. Its church meets wherever men lift festive bowls to toast joys remembered or anticipated. Its liturgy is the exuberant enactment of fantasy before the eyes of a prosaic world. Its God is the often unspoken ground for refusing to be cowed into timidity or resignation by mere facts.

This gift of comic hope is not something on which religious people hold a monopoly. They share it with all sorts and conditions of men. But it may be the special responsibility of men of faith to nourish this gift, to celebrate this sense of comic hope, and to demonstrate it. It could conceivably disappear, and where laughter and hope have disappeared man has ceased to be man.

Coda

Coda

The Feast of Fools flourished during a period when people had a well-developed capacity for festivity and fantasy. We need to develop that capacity again today. We cannot and should not try to resuscitate the jesters and gargoyles of the Middle Ages. But neither need we exclude medieval man entirely from our consciousness. We can benefit from the experience of that time to enrich and vitalize our own, just as we can learn from other historical epochs and other civilizations.

What the medieval period had was a kind of festivity which related men to history and bound them to each other in a single community. Neither national holidays nor periodic but empty "long weekends" had yet appeared to divide and trivialize human celebration. Today we need a rebirth of festivity that will make us part of a larger history than they knew and will link us to an immensely expanded world community. Our survival as a species may depend in part on whether such authentically worldwide festivals, with their symbols of a single global community, emerge among us.

The Middle Ages also displayed a capacity for fantasy that, although it became more constricted during the industrial centuries, may now be staging a comeback. Medieval man, for all his limitations, placed a higher value on imagination than we do. He could make believe more easily. His saints and holy people did things we would not permit. Would St. Francis and St. Theresa escape incarceration, at least for purposes of observation, in the modern world? We need fantasy today. Can we make a more secure place for it in our cognitively overdeveloped schools? Can we mold a universal symbolism within which we can both fantasize and still communicate? Can we become less doctrinaire about what constitutes "mental health" and encourage a much more generous range of life styles? A rebirth of fantasy need not result in the death of rational thought. Both belong in any healthy culture.

Will we make it? Will we move into this world of revitalized celebration and creative imagination? Or will we destroy ourselves with nuclear bombs or man-made plagues? Or will we survive as a precarious planet where a small affluent elite perches fearfully on the top of three continents of hungry peons? Or will we all end up in a subhuman world of efficiently lobotomized robots?

The world symbolized by the Feast of Fools is neither *Walden Two* nor *1984*. It is much more heterogeneous, messier, more sensuous, more variegated, more venturesome, more playful. It is a world for which a fiesta or even a love-in is a better symbol than a computer or a rocket. Technology need not be the enemy of the spirit in the modern world. But it should be a means to man's human fulfillment, not the symbol or goal of that fulfillment itself.

When we honestly ask ourselves whether we can have such a life-affirming world, we must move beyond mere optimism or pessimism, for the empirical evidence is either mixed or unfavorable. But we can hope. Hope in the religious sense rests in part on nonempirical grounds. Christian hope suggests that man is destined for a City. It is not just any city, however. If we take the Gospel images as well as the symbols of the book of Revelation into consideration, it is not only a City where injustice is abolished and there is no more crying. It is a city in which a delightful wedding feast is in progress, where the laughter rings out, the dance has just begun, and the best wine is still to be served.

Appendix

Appendix: Some Relevant Theological Currents

I turn now to a discussion of some matters that, although they will be of considerable interest to some readers, will be of indifference to others: the theological and intellectual currents that were influencing me as I wrote this book, and how it is related to them. I will mention eight of them.

(1) *Theology and experience.* Theology is now rapidly emerging from a nearly half-century-long period in which any attention to actual human experience was derogated. The history especially of Protestant theology from the publication of Karl Barth's *Epistle to the Romans* in the early 1920's up to the most recent years tells the story of the rediscovery of biblical and Reformation objectivity. Barth insisted, especially in his early years, that subjectivity and human experience provided at best a deceptive basis for faith and a mercurial object for theology.[1] The theologian, he insisted, must focus on the Word of God. Friedrich Schleiermacher, the great nineteenth-century theologian of experience, fell into disrepute. What was often somewhat arrogantly called "Biblical" theology became popular and no one paid much attention to human experience, religious or otherwise.

Now all that is changing. Several recent influential works in theology have, in one way or another, rescued experience from its ignominious banishment. Leslie Dewart, in *The Future of Belief*[2] and again in *The Foundations of Belief* argues that modern man's experience of his own autonomy and power must be taken into consideration by theology. Some theologians have begun to examine how people *actually* talk about God and faith instead of how they are *supposed* to. The death-of-God thinkers base their assertions on a probing of contemporary man's cultural incapacity for God. More recently still, Gregory Baum has attempted to construct a modern apologetic based on the exposition of man's "depth experiences," an approach that harks back to the French Catholic philosopher Maurice Blondel (1861–1949).[3]

Experience, despite the difficulty of analyzing and clarifying it, has once again become a worthy object of theological discussion. With this change, those thinkers who have given a larger place to human experience are also being read more sympathetically. Schleiermacher was eloquently revived by Richard R. Niebuhr in 1964 in his *Schleiermacher: On Christ and Religion*.[4] Paul Lehmann devoted a section in his *Ethics in a Christian Context* to the nearly forgotten (by theologians) William James.[5] *The Varieties of Religious Experience* which James published in 1902 is being read again. Even Ralph Waldo Emerson, who in 1838 warned Harvard Divinity School students that experience must displace inherited dogma in their lives, has once again found an audience. Experience is back as a legitimate subject of theological work. In this book I accept this tendency and examine festivity and fantasy primarily as human experiences, albeit with far-reaching religious significance.

(2) *Theology of Culture*. With the death of Paul Tillich the most brilliant practitioner of the theology of culture departed from the scene. No single figure has appeared to claim his place as the principal theological interpreter of such cultural forms as painting, music, architecture, and dance. Still, the work of the theology of culture has continued. Its representatives, however, tend to specialize in one or two fields of cultural creation and avoid for the most part trying to cover the whole. Nathan Scott[6] and Maynard Kaufman work mainly on literature and poetry. William Lynch focuses on film. Tom Driver specializes in theatre.[7] Only Walter Ong makes much of an attempt to pull the whole range of cultural artifacts into a single inclusive theological interpretation.

The main problem with most of what is written today in

theology of culture is that it rarely makes any connection between cultural creations and political action. It fails to span the gap between symbol and society. We lack in theology a person who, like George Steiner, Susan Sontag, George Lukacs, or Irving Howe, tries consistently to relate the aesthetic to the political realm. Despite the excellent writing done in theology of culture, very little of it enriches the thinking of theological ethics.

Maybe the reason we often fail to make this connection in America is that we are rightly suspicious of the political exploitation of art. But the relation between culture and politics need not always be negative. Man's decisions are shaped and influenced by the symbols that define his reality and bestow on him his identity. In theological ethics today we are rightly concerned with moral argument and the nature of ethical discourse. We do not often pause, however, to examine the cultural orientations that determine even the question of what is and what is not an ethical choice. In this book I try at points to span this gap and to discuss the wider symbolic context within which moral reasoning and political action proceed.

The German word "Kulturpolitik" has no real equivalent in English. The fact that it does not suggests that some Europeans possess categories for relating cultural analysis to political possibility that we lack. It is my hope that in the future the theology of culture and theological ethics can benefit each other more than they have in the past. We know songs and symbols have important political significance. We know there is some relation between aesthetic and political modes. We know the images of life conveyed by films and books and even by clothes and dance styles influence the political life of a society and vice versa. This book aims in part at the intersection between theology of culture and ethics. It draws on both gratefully, but it suggests no particularly original way in which the two can be drawn closer together. That remains an important unsolved problem in theology.

(3) *Theology and Religion.* Along with the "neo-orthodox"

suspicion for experience there came a mood of near contempt for what was called "religion." Barth once wrote that Jesus Christ is the end of religion. Bonhoeffer called for a "non-religious interpretation of the Gospel," and several people have taken up his challenge. Even Tillich once said that the first word of theology must always be a word against religion.

Although none of these men was ever as one-sidedly "anti-religious" as some of their disciples turned out to be, and although they meant a variety of sometimes very subtle things when they talked about "religion," still this criticism of religion by theology had a certain damaging effect. For one thing, the interest both in the history of religion and in comparative religion declined markedly during the period of their influence and has only now begun to reemerge. The same was true for the psychology of religion and the philosophy of religion. Rather, the popular subjects during this period were Bible, history of Christian thought, theology, and ethics. "Religion" became a word that was almost as deeply suspect as "experience," and when put together they became virtually anathema.

Now all of that has changed. Theologians today are not afraid to talk about "religion" anymore, even about *homo religiosus*. Courses in the psychology of religion and comparative religion are very popular. Whatever the final resolution of the question of whether Christianity is or is not a "religion" may be, there is less tendency now to see the relationship solely in negative terms.

(4) *The Phenomenological Method.* Edmund Husserl (1859-1938) made one of the most important contributions to modern philosophy when he suggested that thinkers should lay aside mere speculation and deduction and should concentrate instead on the careful description of human consciousness. By giving attention to the "phenomenon itself," Husserl contended, a philosopher can discover the structures of experience and thus make a real contribution. He insisted that in this rigorous examination of the objects of human consciousness, no pre-

conceptions whatever about what is "real" or "unreal" should be allowed. This meant that such previously taboo subjects as anxiety, boredom, joy, and prayer became perfectly legitimate objects of disciplined philosophical analysis.

Husserl's method, which resembles to some extent Kierkegaard's approach in some of his books, influenced enormously the thought of Jean-Paul Sartre, Martin Heidegger, and Karl Jaspers. Through them it touched the contemporary "existentialist" movement. More recently Husserl's method was greatly refined by the late French thinker Maurice Merleau-Ponty in his *Phenomenology of Perception*.[8] Adaptations of the phenomenological method have been used with considerable success in theology by Paul Tillich and Paul Ricoeur. They proceed on the sound assumption that a theologically informed intelligence can use this method to reveal the structure and significance of those aspects of consciousness that have a particularly salient importance for theology.

In this book, although I have used certain features of the phenomenological approach in my discussion, for example, of festivity, by and large I have utilized the results of other people's phenomenological investigations. This is especially true of the sections on fantasy. Often I have combined their insights with historical and sociological ones in my treatment. Whatever the success of the enterprise in the present book, I am convinced that the use of the phenomenological method holds rich promise for theology in the future.

(5) *Roman Catholic Contribution.* There was a time not long ago when Protestant theologians assigned the writings of Catholics theologians to their students mainly so they would know "what Catholics are thinking" about an issue. This is simply no longer the case. Today Catholic and non-Catholic theologians write, for the most part, within the same arena of issues. There is hardly an important topic in the current theological discussion to which both Catholics and others have not made a significant contribution. One simply cannot "cover"

such topics as eschatology, ecclesiology, or apologetics without references respectively to Johannes Metz, Hans Küng, or Gregory Baum. Of course, traces of a particular tradition remain visible in the approach these men take, and it probably always should. More and more, however, theology is becoming authentically "ecumenical" in its style and procedure. Theologians from a particular tradition draw on other traditions where it will help clarify or illuminate a problem.

For myself, I like to think of the work I do as ecumenical theology, not because it deals with a limited number of overworked "ecumenical" questions (papacy, apostolic succession, grace and works, and so forth) but because it draws on sources without reference to ecclesiastical boundaries. In this book in particular it would have been impossible to remain narrowly "Protestant" since almost all the best literature on festivity is by Catholics (Hugo Rahner, Josef Pieper, and Romano Guardini are the most significant). In fact, it is interesting to speculate on why there is such a paucity of Protestant material on festivity and celebration. I am tempted to think it is because of the overemphasis on work ethics in some strains of Protestantism. In any case, anyone comparing the theological sources of my inspiration for this book with those of *The Secular City* cannot help noticing how much more heavily I rely here on Catholic writers. This should be no surprise, however. It is happening to all of us. Before too much longer it will not even be a sufficiently interesting point to bring up.

One special point deserves mention in this regard. In the past the Catholic theology of culture often has been handicapped in its evaluation of the present by a nostalgic preference for the Middle Ages. For the most part this is no longer the case. In fact, some Catholic theologians like Johannes Metz sometimes seem to go to extreme lengths in their enthusiasm for the modern world. I am not homesick for the great medieval synthesis. Although the title of this book comes from a medieval festival, I realize all too well that the medieval achievement may not have been all its admirers claim. In any case there is no way back.

Still, I cannot pretend to have an unconditional enthusiasm for the technopolitan world, nor to feel that the medieval period was a total loss. If the ecumenical conversation has allowed Catholics to move away from their wistful longings for the thirteenth century, maybe it can help Protestants see that there were indeed some features of medieval life worth learning from. In this book I mention two of them: festivity and fantasy. There may be others. But I realize full well they can only be reappropriated in a radically transformed and contemporized form. Still, a dash of affection for the Middle Ages may not hurt us after all. It corrects our temporal provincialism just as an interest in other cultures corrects our geographical narrowness. Besides, an age that produced St. Francis, the troubadours, and those raucous student drinking songs cannot be all bad.

(6) *The Challenge of Sociology.* The dialogue between theology and the sociology of religion is approaching a promising new threshold. There was once a period when social scientists were feared by theologians as muckrakers bent on exposing things about religious institutions and practices that might better have been kept in the closet. That was the "antagonism" phase. There followed a period in which churchmen became fascinated with the utilization of sociological techniques for learning more about their parishes and even for sizing-up the "market" for religion. That was the "parish survey" phase. Now, however, a new and more intellectually promising stage in the relationship has started.

Sociologists of religion, especially those who work within a broad historical setting and with precise conceptual tools, are stimulating theologians to rethink the entire structure and significance of religion. They do so because they focus rather relentlessly not on what religion *says* it does for people but on what its *actual* impact is. Thus, they expose the gap between reality and institutional ideology in theology. But this is more than mere exposé. If, for example, sociologists can clarify what symbols really mean to people, and what they are seeking when they explore religious ideas, those whose job it is to clarify and refine religious doctrines can hardly afford to remain uninterested.

Three contemporary sociologists of religion in particular pose questions which theology can ill afford to neglect: Robert Bellah, Peter Berger, and Thomas Luckmann. Robert Bellah has described what he calls the "civil religion of America." [9] Among other things he examines the inaugural addresses of all the American Presidents in order to trace out some coherent nonchurch religion in American history. He succeeds remarkably well in doing so. There are two contributions, in particular, that I think Bellah's essay makes to theology. First, he reminds us that if we fasten only on "church religion" in our work we are missing a good deal of what must be called "religion" today. If theology is to religion what, say, criticism is to literature; then, if Bellah is right, the theologian must widen his sights. It was partly in response to Bellah's work and other like it that I have been emboldened as a theologian to examine such essentially nonecclesial phenomena as festivity and fantasy. Second, Bellah demonstrates in his examination of civil religion how the study of ceremonial occasions can uncover values and beliefs that ordinarily remain unexpressed. The holiday or festival is just such an occasion.

Another sociologist, Peter Berger, in his most recent book *A Rumor of Angels* challenges theologians to examine what he calls the "signals of transcendence" that are discoverable even in modern secularized industrial society.[10] These clues are found in those perennial human experiences for which there is no measurable empirical basis. Berger himself mentions play, hope, our sense for order, for evil, and for the comic. I wrote my discussion on play and the comic in the last chapter of this book before I read Berger's book, and I am sure there is much more to be done on these subjects. Maybe, however, man's perennial need to celebrate and his irrepressible bent for fantasy may also be "clues to transcendence." I rather believe they are. In any case, Berger's work stimulates theology to move in the direction of experience analysis, not just of exegesis.

Finally, Thomas Luckmann states very explicitly and at greater length some of the same challenges to theology that also come from Bellah's work. In his book *The Invisible Religion* he argues that religion in industrial societies is no longer the monopoly of specialized religious institutions.[11] Many different agencies mediate values and meanings today, and the individual can pick, choose, or combine. Like Bellah, Luckmann makes it difficult for a theologian who concerns himself exclusively with church religion to be taken very seriously. Just as education is not by any means confined to schools, so religion cannot be equated with what goes on in churches. Any theologian must today be something of a theologian of culture.

Sociologists not only keep theologians honest. They also raise conceptual issues and theoretical problems that theologians avoid at their peril. I have tried in this book to maintain a conversation with sociology throughout. If I have not succeeded it is not because I think this contact is not important.

(7) *Symbol Analysis.* Symbol is a "hinge category." It is one of those notions that cuts across traditional disciplinary lines since the analysis of symbols cannot be contained by any one academic department. Psychologists, sometimes using projective techniques, analyze the significance of symbols for the person. Anthropologists study the way symbols function in a culture. Literary critics dissect the symbols in a poem or a novel. Architects and city planners concern themselves with the symbolic significance of focal places, of buildings and monuments, and of the various ways space is arranged. Students of religion cannot help studying the gestures and objects of religious worship and thought.

My own thinking has been influenced by people who study symbols from many different perspectives. I have often wished we had a more unified method for the thorough analysis of symbols and, although "symbology" is a word, unfortunately no rigorous approach to the study of symbols has yet been devised. In this book "The Feast of Fools" is obviously a symbol, not just a nearly forgotten medieval custom. But that is not so unusual. Since a symbol is something that "points beyond itself" as Tillich used to say, something that stands for something more than its mere perceptual content, other similar occasions have also served as symbols before. Games, banquets, revels, fairs—all have served symbolic functions.

The American social scientist Lloyd Warner, who began his work with the Murngin in Central Australia and ended it by studying the people of Newburyport, Massachusetts, discovered early in his career that festive occasions had enormous symbolic significance for the participants. In Australia he studied the "kunapipi," the annual celebrative gathering of the tribe, and found in it a rich source of information on what the Murngin believed and who they were. In Newburyport, which he called "Yankee City," Warner studied, among other things, the town's 200th anniversary celebration and the annual Memorial Day activities. His work proves to me that the symbolic analysis of holidays is immensely rewarding. In this book, although I remain aware of the contribution he made and the similar contributions made by others, my own analysis of cultural symbols remains at a very preliminary level. Nevertheless, the tools for this sort of analysis are being developed very quickly both by the so-called "structuralists" such as Lévi-Strauss, and by those who combine features of ethnological and linguistic analysis in examining speech and gesture behavior. This also represents a tendency with which theology would be well advised to keep in close touch.

(8) *Comparative Religion.* Closely related to the return of interest in religious experience and the refinement of the

phenomenological method is the massive new enthusiasm for the study of what are sometimes provincially described as "non-Christian religions." As my colleague Raymond Pannikar has so forcefully reminded me in personal conversation, this designation is both arrogant and unscientific. It bespeaks a kind of Western Christian condescension, and it lumps together so many different things as to be totally useless as a category. Regardless of what we call it, however, the study of the faiths of other men is increasingly important.

The great religious systems of the world have become an interesting problem for Christian theology only comparatively recently in its history, mostly in the modern period. In recent decades, due again to the enormous emphasis on so-called "kerygmatic" or biblical theology, the number of people doing careful theological reflection on the world religions waned. Such scholars as Mircea Eliade and my own colleague Wilfred Cantwell Smith never stopped their work during this period of course. But many people viewed what they were doing as very far from the center of the theological conversation. One of the few people who managed to span the poles of dialectical theology and world religion was Hendrik Kraemer, but his perspective never found much favor with the comparativists themselves.

Today there is hardly anything that interests theological students more than the study of comparative religion and the effort to evolve a Christian understanding of the faiths of other men. There are many reasons for this change. One is the intrusion of the "Third World" into the consciousness of Western man in the years since World War II. Asia and Africa are no longer distant mysteries but neighbors. Students travel more today, see films from all around the world, meet overseas students on their own campuses. Also, mainly in the last two decades, a wide variety of different forms of Eastern religious practices have made their way to American shores. Zen Buddhism has ceased to be a mere fad. It is taken seriously as a faith by large numbers of people, as are other religious perspectives originating in the Orient.

I have done very little in this book to include a comparative dimension. In a way I regret it because I am sure it would have strengthened my thesis immensely. I avoided doing it because I have become aware how demanding it is to do such a job well, especially when one is not prepared for it in his training. One possible way to compare faiths would be to compare the various festivals of faith—Ramadan, Holi, Christmas, Passover. I have not done this in the present book, but I am convinced that the approach I have taken here would work well on a comparative basis, and that is what is important. Just as any future theology must use a method which makes a place for the analysis of experience, phenomenologically and in other ways, and just as it must draw on all the resources of the Christian tradition, such a theology must also be open in principle to the insights that can be gained from a comparative investigation.

These are the movements in current theological thinking within which I attempt to steer my bark. No one of them qualifies as a "movement." The only tendencies that even vaguely deserve this title today are the quiescent radical-theology movement and the just appearing theology of hope.

Some will wonder whether the approach of this book attempts to revive some elements of Paul Tillich's "method of correlation." It does not. Tillich's method proved to be, in his hands, a remarkably productive tool. He began by analyzing the questions implicit in culture and then went on to show how the "symbols of faith" correlate with these questions. In my view the relation between faith and culture is a more complex one. Faith does not always answer the questions posed by human existence; it sometimes raises questions of its own. And the cultures into which human existence organizes itself sometimes give answers, however provisional and partial, to the questions raised by faith. The faith-culture interaction is further complicated by the fact that faith, as Tillich said, must always express itself through cultural forms, and all culture is to some extent the vehicle of some element of faith.

This means that the theologian of culture cannot shift back and forth from his role as cultural analyst to his role as theological exegete as smoothly as Tillich could, or thought he could. The theologian of culture makes use of a variety of techniques—historical, social scientific, phenomenological—but his reading of a situation is informed at all times by his knowledge of theology. He writes quite self-consciously from a particular perspective and makes no false claims to sheer objectivity. His theological perspective colors everything from his selection of the topic, to his choice of sources, to his arrangement of the material and his decisions about emphasis and style. He tries to be conscious of his starting point and not to let his theology distort the picture. But he recognizes that no one writes without premises or a point of view. How to be aware of one's premises without being paralyzed by them remains one of the most persistent and fascinating problems with which any writer, theological or otherwise, must learn to contend.

Notes

Notes

Introduction

"Whitsunday in Kirchstetten" by W. H. Auden can be found in *About the House* (New York: Random House, 1965). © Copyright 1965 by W. H. Auden.

For a splendid article on the relation between philosophy and imagination, see David L. Norton, "Philosophy and Imagination" in *The Centennial Review*, Fall 1968. See also George Pitcher's essay "Wittgenstein, Nonsense and Lewis Carroll" in K. T. Fann, *Ludwig Wittgenstein: The Man and His Philosophy* (New York: Dell, 1967), pp. 315–335. He shows how both of these men in very different ways, were fascinated by fantasy, imaginary words, and situations.

For the relation of Puritanism to modern science, see Robert Merton's famous essays in *Social Theory and Social Structure* (Glencoe, Ill.: Free Press, 1956).

For scholasticism's contribution, see Alfred North Whitehead, *Science and the Modern World* (New York: Macmillan, 1926).

For Christianity's role in initiating secularization, see Harvey Cox, *The Secular City* (New York: Macmillan, 1965); Friedrich Gogarten, *Verhängnis und Hoffnung der Neuzeit* (Stuttgart: Vorwerk, 1953); Johannes Baptist Metz, *Zur Theologie der Welt* (Mainz: Matthias Grünewald Verlag, 1968); and Joachim Friese, *Die Säkularisierte Welt* (Frankfurt: Schulte-Bulmke, 1967). The subtitle of Friese's book is "Triumph or Tragedy of Christian Cultural History." He shows both the causative role of Christianity in secularization and the ambiguous outcome of the process. John Macquarrie, *New Directions in Theology Today*, vol. III: *God and Secularity* (Philadelphia: Westminster, 1967) is a thoughtful and largely critical examination of such "theologians of the secular" as Dietrich Bonhoeffer, Ronald Gregor-Smith, John A. T. Robinson, and myself. To my mind Macquarrie underestimates the problems posed for theism by our contemporary sensibility, but his descriptions of the positions of those he criticizes are usually very accurate. A much more positive evaluation of many of the same writers is given by the late Robert L. Richard, S.J., in his *Secularization Theology* (New York: Herder and Herder, 1967). Finally, for a capable defense of a view of Christianity that laments the loss of Christendom, and therefore laments any kind of secularization, see Jean Danielou, *Prayer as a Political Problem*, J. R. Kirwan, ed. (New York: Sheed and Ward, 1965), originally published as *L'Oraison problème politique* (Paris: Fayard, 1965).

1. Festivity: The Ingredients

The social scientific literature on festivity shades into the discussion of ritual and will be discussed below in the notes to Chapter 5. A classic work in the psychological and anthropological analysis of festivals, especially of those that have become known as the "saturnalia" type, is Ernest Crawley, *The Mystic Rose* (London: Edward T. Besterman, 1927). Carl Kerényi discusses the role of festivals in Greek and Roman religion in *The Religions of the Greeks and Romans* (London: Thames and Hudson, 1962), especially in chapter 2. Also relevant to later sections of this book are Kerényi's chapters on "Theoria" and "The Laughter of the Gods." Walter F. Otto, *Dionysus: Myth and Cult,* Robert B. Palmer, trans. (Bloomington: Indiana University Press, 1965) remains to my mind the most readable account of that strange and fascinating god. See especially his excellent chapter on "Pandemonium and Silence."

Lloyd W. Warner has an excellent description of "kunapipi," the central festival of the central Australian Murngin in his *A Black Civilization: A Social Study of an Australian Tribe* (New York: Harper, 1937). He also includes a description and analysis of the tercentenary celebration in "Yankee City" in his *The Living and the Dead* (New Haven: Yale University Press, 1959), volume V in the Yankee City series.

Festivals and feasts were also important in ancient Judaism. Besides the Sabbath itself, there were such great national festivals as Passover, Sukkoth (the Feast of Ingathering), and later, Purim and Hanukkah. Photeine P. Bourboulis has written an excellent monograph entitled *Ancient Festivals of the "Saturnalia" Type* (*Hellenica* supplement no. 16, published by Thessalonika in 1964). He deals with Babylonian, Hittite, and Traco-phrygian examples of saturnalia.

For the theology of celebration I have relied mainly on Hugo Rahner, *Man at Play* (New York: Herder and Herder, 1967) and Josef Pieper, *In Tune With the World: A Theory of Festivity,* Richard and Clara Winston, trans. (New York: Harcourt, Brace, 1965). For Roger Caillois, see *Man, Play and Games,* Meyer Barash, trans. (Glencoe, Ill.: Free Press, 1961). The Roman Catholic theologian Frederic Debuyst, O.S.B., includes a chapter on celebration in his *Modern Architecture and Christian Celebration,* Ecumenical Studies in Worship, no. 18 (London: Lutterworth Press, 1968). J. A. Jungmann has an article entitled "Das Kirliche Fest nach Idee und Grenze" in *Verkündigung und Glaube: Festgabe für Franz X. Arnold* (Freiburg: Verlag Herder, 1958). *Kirche in der Zeit* (Düsseldorf), a Protestant journal of theology, published some articles on holidays and celebration in its volume XII in 1957. Karl Barth has a discussion of the same subject in his *Church Dogmatics* (Edinburgh: T. & T. Clark, 1961), vol. III, part 4, section 53, on "The Holy Day."

The best concise critical bibliography I have found on festivity is in E. O. James, *Seasonal Feasts and Festivals* (New York: Barnes & Noble, 1963).

1. Roger Caillois, "Théorie de la fête," in *Nouvelle révue française,* 53 (1939). This essay was later included by Caillois in his book *Man and the Sacred,* Meyer Barash, trans. (Glencoe, Ill.: Free Press, 1959).

2. Pieper, p. 23.

3. Friedrich Nietzsche, *The Will to Power,* Walter Kaufmann and R. J. Hollingdale, trans. (New York: Random House, 1967).

4. Gerardus van der Leeuw, *Sacred and Profane Beauty: The Holy in Art* (New York: Holt, Rinehart, 1963).

5. Johan Huizinga, *Homo Ludens: A Study of the Play Element in Culture* (Boston: Beacon Press, 1955).

6. Pieper, p. 3.

7. Pieper, p. 7.

8. F. S. C. Northrop, *The Meeting of East and West: An Inquiry Concerning World Understanding* (New York: Macmillan, 1946), p. 54.

9. Northrop, p. 37.

10. Jean Cocteau, "On Frivolity," in *The Journals of Jean Cocteau,* Wallace Fowlie ed. and trans. (New York: Criterion Books, 1956), pp. 201–206.

11. Cocteau, p. 202.

2. Festivity and the Death of God

For the death-of-God controversy the bibliographical references are numberless. See especially, however, T. J. J. Altizer, *The Gospel of Christian Atheism* (Philadelphia: Westminster, 1966); William Hamilton and T. J. J. Altizer, *Radical Theology and the Death of God* (Indianapolis: Bobbs Merrill, 1966); William Hamilton, "The Death of God Theology" in W. R. Miller, ed., *The New Christianity* (New York: Delacorte Press, 1967), originally published in *The Christian Scholar,* Spring 1965. The best assessment of the controversy is found in Thomas Ogletree, *The Death of God Controversy* (New York: Abingdon, 1966).

For Mircea Eliade's position see his fascinating final chapter entitled "The Terror of History" in *Cosmos and History* (New York: Harper, 1959). Kaufman's argument is eloquently advanced in his essay "Post Christian Aspects of the Radical Theology" in T. J. J.

Altizer, ed., *Toward a New Christianity* (New York: Harcourt, Brace, 1967). For an excellent recent book on this whole subject, see John Lukacs, *Historical Consciousness or the Remembered Past* (New York: Harper, 1968).

In the recent theological discussion about history and history-making there are some thinkers who would not agree with my summary of the issue. Friedrich Gogarten insists there is "nothing but history," that is, that for Christianity all of reality has become history. History "has become the problem of reality" ("Theology and History" in Robert Funk and Gerhard Ebeling, eds., *History and Hermeneutic* [New York: Harper, 1967]). The late Carl Michaelson also would probably have rejected my assertion that reality is not exhausted by history. In a spirited defense of historicism in *Worldly Theology* (New York: Scribner, 1967) he says that history cannot be treated as "one more regional ontology" because it is *not* "one among several," but "the horizon of every area of investigation." History is "an horizon so inescapable that being itself is a derivative of history" (pp. 104–105).

Michaelson published those words in 1963, however, and more recent theologies of history have not put the matter so unqualifiedly. Wolfhart Pannenberg, for example, can argue that the world is history, a "succession of events" and not a "given order of things," but do so in a way that honors instead of denigrating the ontological quest. See his essay in James M. Robinson, ed., *New Frontiers in Theology,* vol. III: *Theology as History* (New York: Harper, 1967), pp. 132, 133.

For Antonin Artaud see his *The Theatre and Its Double* (New York: Grove Press, 1958). See also the *Antonin Artaud Anthology,* Jack Hirschman, ed. (San Francisco: City Lights Books, 1965). In her very recent book *Antonin Artaud: Man of Vision* (New York: David Lewis, 1969), Betina L. Knapp contends that neither Genêt, Ionesco, Pinter, or Weiss would have been possible without Artaud's inspiration. Though this may lean toward a slight overestimation of his influence, Knapp helps restore Artaud to something like the place he deserves in the history of Western theatre. She also gives us a useful account of the relation between Artaud's own tragic life and his dramatic theories.

For John Cage, see especially *Silence: Selected Lectures and Writings* (Middletown: Wesleyan University Press, 1961).

Bread and Wine can be found in Michael Hamburger, ed., *Hölderlin* (New York: Pantheon, 1952). Copyright 1952 by Pantheon Books Inc.

1. Mircea Eliade, *Cosmos and History* (New York: Harper, 1959).

2. Pierre Teilhard de Chardin, *The Divine Milieu* (New York: Harper, 1960). It first appeared in Paris as *Le Milieu divin* in 1957.

3. T. S. Eliot, "The Dry Salvages," in the *Four Quartets* (New York: Harcourt, Brace, 1943), p. 27. Copyright, 1943, by T. S. Eliot.

4. Richard L. Rubenstein, *After Auschwitz* (New York: Bobbs Merrill, 1966).

5. Rubeinstein's argument is also advanced in a different form by such thinkers as Mircea Eliade, Thomas J. J. Altizer, and Maynard Kaufman.

6. Norman O. Brown is the author of *Life Against Death* (Middletown: Wesleyan University Press, 1959) and *Love's Body* (New York: Random House, 1966).

7. Brown, *Life Against Death*, p. 19.

8. Lynn White, Jr., "On Intellectual Gloom," in *The American Scholar*, 35 (Spring 1966), p. 224.

9. *Ibid.*

10. Hayden V. White, "The Burden of History," in *History and Theory*, 5, no. 2 (1966), p. 115.

11. Artaud, *The Theatre and Its Double*, p. 74.

12. Artaud, p. 74.

13. Artaud, p. 80. (Italics mine)

14. Artaud, p. 78.

15. Nicola Chiaromonte, "Antonin Artaud," in *Encounter*, 28 (August 1967), p. 46.

16. Friedrich Nietzsche, "The Gay Science" in *The Portable Nietzsche*, Walter Kaufmann, ed. (New York: Viking, 1954), p. 96.

17. Jacob Burckhardt, *The Civilization of the Rennaissance in Italy* (New York: Harper, 1958), pp. 18–19.

18. Herbert Read, *Icon and Idea: The Function of Art in the Development of Human Consciousness* (New York: Schocken, 1965).

19. Michael Polanyi, *The Tacit Dimension* (Garden City, N. Y.: Doubleday, 1966).

3. A Dance Before The Lord

1. E. Louis Backman, *Religious Dances in the Christian Church and in Popular Medicine* (London: Allen & Unwin, 1952). Also for the place of dance in worship, see Margaret Fisk Taylor, *A Time to Dance: Symbolic Movement in Worship* (Philadelphia: United Church Press, 1967); "Religion and the Dance," a report of a consultation on the dance sponsored by the Department of Worship and the Arts, National Council of Churches of Christ, on November 16, 1960.

2. As quoted in Backman, p. 19. For the reference to Clement of Alexandria, see vol. II of the *Ante-Nicene Fathers* (New York: Christian Literature Co., 1893), p. 205. This is chapter XII of Clement's "Exhortation to the Heathen." The passage is particularly important because in it Clement seems to be contrasting Christian worship and initiation to that of the Maenades, and other Bacchic rites. He writes, "Come, O Madman, not leaning on the thyrsus [the vine-crowned staff associated with Bacchus], not crowned with ivy; throw away the mitre, throw away the fawn-skin . . ." But he then goes on to mention dancing, torches, and the choir of angels. Backman believes the passage describes a ring dance around the altar which the novitiate performed not only with the other novitiates but also with the angels.

3. For Eusebius, see *The Essential Eusebius* in a new translation by Colm Luibhéid (New York: New American Library, 1966), p. 181. See also Backman, p. 23.

4. As quoted in Backman, p. 25. The translation of St. Basil's "Sermon on Drunkenness" from which this excerpt is taken is supplied by Backman himself. The original can be found in *Basilii Opera Omnia, tomus tertius*; vol. 31 of the *Patrologia Graeca*, J. P. Migne, ed. (Paris, 1857), cols. 443–464.

5. E. R. Dodds, "Maenadism," in *The Greeks and the Irrational* (Boston: Beacon Press, 1957), p. 279, n. 9.

6. Alan Walker, "Where Pentecostalism is Mushrooming" in *Christian Century*, 85 (January 17, 1968), p. 81.

7. Dodds, p. 272.

8. Paul Valery, as quoted by Christopher Larkin in *Federation News,* no. 1, published by the World Student Christian Federation in Geneva, Switzerland (1967), p. 7.

9. Michael Novak: "The Underground Church" in *Saturday Evening Post,* December 28, 1968.

10. William Birmingham, "The Eroticization of Liturgy," in *Continuum* (Winter 1968) p. 734.

11. The claim that some people can dance a prayer who might not be able to say one is not a figure of speech. It recognizes, as recent analysts have, that dance is not a way of expressing through bodily movement an idea or insight which is first thought in words or images. Dance is literally thinking with the body, a form of expression and symbolization which, though long overlooked as such in our society, is now being discussed again. See Maxine Sheets, *The Phenomenology of Dance* (Madison: University of Wisconsin Press, 1966.)

12. Quoted in Gerardus van der Leeuw, *Sacred and Profane Beauty: The Holy in Art* (New York: Holt, Rinehart, 1963), p. 30.

Notes

4. Fantasy: The Ingredients

The works on imagination and fantasy are so numerous that the following is only a personal selection. I begin with *Illusions* by André Maurois (New York: Columbia University Press, 1968), the text of the George T. Pegram Lectures. For a thorough survey of one crucial period see Edward C. Kollman, "Studies in the Modern Theory of Imagination with Especial Reference to its Historical Development from the Renaissance to Kant." It is an unpublished PhD dissertation, dated 1950, available at Widener Library, Harvard University. A previous period is covered by Murray Bundy, *The Theory of Imagination in Classical and Medieval Thought* (Urbana: University of Illinois Press, 1927). Jean Paul Sartre has written two significant books on the subject: *The Psychology of Imagination* (New York: Philosophical Library, 1948), and *L'Imagination* (Paris: Presses universitaires de France, 1950).

On the theological side nothing for a long time can hope to match Roy L. Hart's comprehensive *Unfinished Man and the Imagination* (New York: Herder and Herder, 1968). I have learned a great deal from it and have profited from the extraordinarily complete bibliographical references in the footnotes. Hart himself gives credit to William F. Lynch, S.J. for his pioneering work in the theology of imagination. See Lynch, *Christ and Apollo: The Dimensions of the Literary Imagination* (New York: Sheed and Ward, 1960) and *Images of Hope: Imagination as Healer of the Hopeless* (Baltimore: Helicon, 1965). An even earlier modern pioneer was Nicholas Berdyaev. See his *The Beginning and the End* which was first published in 1941 and is now available in several editions. Mircea Eliade thinks theologically about "waking dreams" in the fifth chapter of *Myths, Dreams, and Mysteries* (New York: Harper, 1960). In his recent *Dreams, the Dark Speech of the Spirit: A Christian Interpretation* (New York: Doubleday, 1968), Morton T. Kelsey deals with night, or sleeping, dreams which he sharply distinguishes from daydreams (p. 201). He also makes a very sharp distinction between daydreams and fantasies (p. 8). He includes a fascinating appendix with excerpts from Tertullian, Origen, Gregory of Nyssa, and St. Augustine.

See also Leopold Caligor and Rollo May, *Dreams and Symbols: Man's Unconscious Language* (New York: Basic Books, 1968).

The relationship of fantasy to other aspects of life is particularly well discussed by Philip E. Slater in *Microcosm: Structural, Psychological, and Religious Evolution in Groups* (New York: Wiley, 1966). In suggesting that development means capturing portions of "reality" from "fantasy," he warns that this does *not* mean that the realm of fantasy is diminished. "On the contrary," he says, "the brighter the light the deeper the darkness by contrast . . . the greater the areas of dry land the deeper the pools into which the sea must be distributed." By detaching fact from fantasy, he argues that the fantasy is not abolished but "purified and intensified" (p. 145).

The question of what is the proper place of fantasy in human life has also catalyzed a spirited discussion in the sometimes arid field of educational psychology. In his *Fantasy and Feeling in Education* (New York: New York University Press, 1968), Richard Jones has set about correcting, criticizing, and complementing what he believes is an overemphasis on the cognitive aspect of learning in the widely respected views of Jerome S. Bruner. See especially Bruner, *Toward a Theory of Instruction* (Cambridge, Mass.: Harvard University Press, 1966) and *On Knowing: Essays for the Left Hand* (Cambridge, Mass.: Harvard University Press, 1962). Jones claims that if the distinction be made between "iconic," "enactive," and "ratiocinative" modes of representing reality, we do not develop from one to another but must have periodic returns to the first two. He sees certain conflicts between ratiocination and our more basic drives. But he insists that the way to "prevent such excesses of drive tension as can overrule our more civilized intentions is to provide *regular opportunities* (italics mine) for drive satisfaction in enactive and iconic forms" (p. 257). What Jones seems to be advocating here is the periodic occasion of legitimated excess and celebration that we have identified with festivity, and the iconic play we have discussed in terms of ritual. Jones also believes enactive and iconic experiences play a vital role in creativity. They inspire more original work in the more cognitive realm. Jones, in my language, sees festivity and ritual closely linked to fantasy and inventiveness.

George Leonard, *Education and Ecstasy* (New York: Delacorte Press, 1968) carries the discussion still further in his portrait of the schools of A.D. 2000 in which educating the emotions will be accepted as just as important as educating the mind.

1. Herbert Marcuse, *Eros and Civilization* (Boston: Beacon Press, 1955).

2. Lewis Mumford, *The Myth of the Machine* (New York: Harcourt, Brace, 1967).

3. Ray Bradbury, as quoted by Mary Harrington Hall, "A Conversation with Ray Bradbury & Chuck Jones: The Fantasy-Makers," in *Psychology Today*, 1, no. 11 (April 1968), pp. 28–37, 70.

4. Thomas S. Kuhn, *The Structure of Scientific Revolutions* (Chicago: University of Chicago Press, 1962).

5. In *Symbolic Wounds* (Glencoe, Ill.: Free Press, 1954), Bruno Bettelheim tells of the important things he learned about young

patients in a mental hospital by carefully observing their behavior at the hospital's Halloween party.

6. Some excellent recent work has challenged the whole concept of mental illness and criticized our society for its punishing attitude toward deviant thought and behavior. See Thomas Szasz, *The Myth of Mental Illness* (New York: Harper, 1961); *Law, Liberty, and Psychiatry* (New York: Macmillan, 1963). Also R. D. Laing, *The Politics of Experience* (New York: Pantheon, 1967).

7. J. R. R. Tolkien, "On Fairy-Stories," *Tree and Leaf* (London: Allen & Unwin, 1964), p. 50.

8. Jerome L. Singer, "The Importance of Daydreaming," *Psychology Today*, 1, no. 11 (April 1968), p. 20.

9. Roger Frétigny and André Virel, *L'Imagerie mentale* (Geneva: Editions de Mont-Blanc, 1968).

10. Frétigny and Virel, p. 19.

5. Fantasy and Religion

There is a large amount of perceptive social scientific material on myth and ritual. In Emile Durkheim's *The Elementary Forms of Religious Life* (New York: Collier, 1961) see especially Book 3. The key essay on the subject was published by Clyde Kluckhohn in the *Harvard Theological Review*, 35 (January 1942), pp. 45–79, entitled "Myths and Rituals, A General Theory." It is republished in William A. Lessa and Evon Z. Vogt: *Reader in Comparative Religion* (New York: Harper, 1965), p. 144. In this same reader we can also find Freud's classic essay on ritual as a form of obsessive act (pp. 197–202). Lessa and Vogt include as well the controversial essay by Claude Lévi-Strauss on "The Structure of Myth" and a response to it by Edmund Leach. Lévi-Strauss, whose work provides one of the few new theoretical departures in the study of myth, is often understood to be saying that the structure of myth can be analyzed without reference to its ritual setting. Though this is certainly true, in my opinion his major contribution is to force us to see ritual in an even wider and more inclusive context than was previously the case. See my "Sociology of Religion in a Post-Religious Era," *The Christian Scholar*, 48 (Spring 1965), pp. 9–26. For another broad approach to ritual, see Erving Goffman, *Interaction Ritual: Essays on Face-to-Face Behavior* (Chicago: Aldine, 1967), a collection of his papers. It documents the patterned and symbolically expressive character of everyday behavior.

The idea that religious worship can be related constructively to human fantasy does not appear very often in English language discussions. There is, however, a somewhat popularized treatment of the subject in German. See Gerhard Schnath, ed., *Fantasie für Gott: Gottesdienste in neuer Gestalt* (Berlin and Stuttgart: Kreuz Verlag, 1965).

1. Josef Pieper, "The Philosophical Act," *Leisure: The Basis of Culture,* Alexander Dru, trans. (New York: Pantheon, 1952), p. 81.
2. See Dom Cuthbert Butler, *Western Mysticism* (New York: Barnes and Noble, 1922) and Norman Cohn, *The Pursuit of the Millennium* (New York: Harper, 1961).
3. Robert Desoille, *Le Rêve eveillé en psychothérapie: Essai sur la fonction de régulation de l'inconscient collectif* (Paris: Presses universitaires de France, 1945).
4. Roger Frétigny and André Virel, *L'Imagerie mentale* (Geneva: Editions de Mont-Blanc, 1968), pp. 271 ff.
5. *The Spiritual Exercises of Saint Ignatius,* Thomas Corbishley, trans. (New York: Kenedy, 1963).

6. Fantasy and Utopia

In his little book *The Story of Utopias* (Boni and Liveright; 1922; re-issued, New York: Viking Press, 1962, with a new introduction by the author), Lewis Mumford begins with Plato and recounts the history of utopian speculation. Despite the new introduction, the book is now somewhat dated, but it remains eminently worth reading. For a more scholarly but also dated source, see Joyce Hertzler, *The History of Utopian Thought* (New York: Macmillan, 1923).

The issue of *Daedalus,* the Journal of the American Academy of Arts and Sciences, for Spring 1965 is entirely devoted to Utopia. See also Glenn Negley and J. Max Patrick, *The Quest for Utopia: An Anthology of Imaginary Societies* (New York: Schuman, 1952) and H. C. Baldry, *Ancient Utopias* (Southampton: University of Southampton, 1956).

For the relation between religious utopianism and social change, see Norman Cohn, *The Pursuit of the Millennium* (New York: Harper, 1961); E. J. Hobsbaum, *Primitive Rebels* (Glencoe, Ill.: Free Press, 1959); and Sylvia L. Thrupp, "Introduction" to *Millennial Dreams in Action: Comparative Studies in Society and History* (The Hague: Mouton, 1962). Martin Buber discusses the religious significance of utopias in *Pathways in Utopia* (London: Routledge & Kegan Paul, 1949). For a critique of certain aspects of utopianism in system designs, see Robert Boguslaw's *The New Utopians* (Englewood Cliffs, N. J.: Prentice Hall, 1965). See also Judith N. Shklar,

After Utopia: The Decline of Political Faith (Princeton: Princeton University Press, 1957).

1. Fred L. Polak, *The Image of the Future* (Dobbs Ferry, N. Y.: Oceana Publications, 1961).
2. Hasan Ozbekhan, "Technology and Man's Future," unpublished paper delivered at the Symposium on the Technological Society, Center for the Study of Democratic Institutions, Santa Barbara, California, December 19–23, 1965.
3. Johannes Baptist Metz, *Zur Theologie der Welt* (Mainz: Matthias-Grünewald Verlag, 1968), p. 93.

7. *Mystics and Militants*

"Under Which Lyre? A Reactionary Tract for the Times" by W. H. Auden, the Phi Beta Kappa poem at Harvard, 1946, can be found in Auden's *Collected Shorter Poems, 1927–1957* (New York: Random House, 1966; London: Faber and Faber, 1966). © Copyright 1966 by W. H. Auden.

1. Carl Kerényi, *The Religion of the Greeks and Romans* (London: Thames & Hudson, 1962), p. 53.
2. Gordon Childe, *What Happened in History* (New York: Penguin, 1946).
3. Morris E. Chafetz, *Liquor: The Servant of Man* (Boston: Little, Brown, 1965).
4. Josef Pieper, *Leisure: The Basis of Culture* (New York: New American Library, 1963), p. 81.
5. Herbert Marcuse, "Actuality of Dialectic," in *Diogenes*, no. 31 (Fall 1960), p. 84.
6. Octavio Paz, *The Labyrinth of Solitude* (New York: Grove Press, 1961). Originally published in 1950 by Caudernos Americanos, Mexico, and expanded in 1959 for the second edition published by the Fondo de Cultura Económica, Mexico, under the title *El Labertino de la Soledad*.
7. Albert Camus, *The Rebel* (New York: Knopf, 1956), p. 296.
8. Camus, p. 302.

8. *Beyond Radical Theology*

For a short bibliography on the death-of-God movement, see the notes to Chapter 2.

For an analysis of the "apocalyptic sensitility" in our culture today, see the following: Frank Kermode, *The Sense of an Ending: Studies in the Theory of Fiction* (New York: Oxford University Press, 1967); George Lichtheim, "The Future" in *Partisan Review,* no. 3 (Summer 1966); and some of the essays in Susan Sontag, *Against Interpretation and Other Essays* (New York: Farrar, Straus, 1966).

For the theology of hope, see Jürgen Moltmann, *Theology of Hope* (New York: Harper, 1967), Gerhard Sauter, *Zukunft und Verheissung* (Zurich: Zwingli Verlag, 1965), Martin Marty and Dean Peerman, *New Theology No. 5* (New York: Macmillan, 1968), and Johannes Metz, "The Church in the World" in T. P. Burke, *The Word in History* (New York: Sheed and Ward, 1966). Also by Metz, see "Friede und Gerechtigkeit, Uberlegungen zu einer Politischen Theologie" in *Civitas-Jahrbuch für Christliche Gesellschaftsordnung* (Mannheim: Pesch-Haus Verlag, 1967) and his essay "Die Verantwortung der Christlichen Gemeinde für dei Planung der Zukunft" in Adolf Exeler, ed., *Die Neue Gemeinde* (Mainz: Matthias-Grunewald Verlag, 1967). Metz edited *Weltverstandie in Glauben* in 1966 (Mainz: Matthias-Grunewald Verlag, 1966).

1. Thomas J. J. Altizer, ed., *Toward a New Christianity* (New York: Harcourt, Brace, 1967), Introduction, p. 13 (italics mine).

2. Altizer, p. 11.

3. Kermode, *The Sense of an Ending.*

4. Very little of Ernst Bloch's work has appeared in English. His masterwork *Das Prinzip Hoffnung,* 3 vols. (Berlin: Aufbau-Verlag, 1959–1960), is difficult but rewarding. Heinze Kimmerle has written a critique of it entitled *Die Zukunftsbedentung der Hoffnung* (Bonn: Bouvier, 1966).

5. Jürgen Moltmann, *Theology of Hope.*

6. Johannes Metz, "The Church in the World," p. 71.

7. Moltmann, p. 15.

8. Moltmann, p. 203.

9. Moltmann, p. 330.

10. Jürgen Moltmann, *Diskussion über Theologie der Hoffnung* (Munich: Chr. Kaiser Verlag, 1967), p. 209.

9. Theology of Juxtaposition

For some of the understanding of perception that underlies this chapter, I am grateful to the insights of Herbert Fingarette, especially as he explains them in *The Self In Transformation* (New York: Harper, 1965).

For a Czech Marxist's view of contemporary religious and theological issues, see Vitezslav Gardavsky, *Gott ist Nicht Ganz Tot* (Munich: Chr. Kaiser Verlag, 1968).

I have argued that juxtaposition bears some resemblance to surrealism. After a long delay we are now beginning to have access to the principal texts of the surrealist movement, thanks to the University of Michigan Press. See André Breton, *Manifestoes of Surrealism,* translated by Richard Seaver and Helen R. Lane (Ann Arbor: University of Michigan Press, 1969). Also Ferdinand Alquié, *The Philosophy of Surrealism* (Ann Arbor: University of Michigan Press, 1965). Herbert S. Gershman has both a book entitled *The Surrealist Revolution in France* and *A Bibliography of the Surrealist Revolution in France* (Ann Arbor: University of Michigan Press, 1969). The same press published J. H. Matthews, *Surrealism and the Novel* in 1966.

1. Leszek Kolakowski, "The Priest and the Jester," in *Dissent,* 9, no. 3 (Summer 1962), p. 233.

2. Morse Peckham, *Man's Rage for Chaos* (Philadelphia: Chilton Books, 1965), p. 40.

3. Susan Sontag, "Happenings," in *Against Interpretation* (New York: Farrar, Straus, 1966), p. 269.

4. Kolakowski, p. 233.

10. *Christ the Harlequin*

I have received a good deal of instruction, both bibliographical and substantive, in the composition of this chapter from David L. Miller, both from a published article entitled "Salvation and the Image of Comedy: Pirandello and Aristophanes," in *Religion and Life* (Summer 1964), and from unpublished manuscripts he has thoughtfully sent me. The manuscript is scheduled for publication by World Publishers, Cleveland and New York, late in 1969. The tentative title is "Of Games and God, Toward a Theology of Play." It is helpful to compare his views on Pirandello with those of the Czech philosopher Bedrich Barmann whose article, "George H. Mead and Luigi Pirandello: Some Parallels Between the Theoretical and Artistic Presentation of the Social Role Concept," in *Social Research,* 34, no. 3 (Autumn 1967), pp. 563–607.

The Comic in Theory and Practice, John J. Enck, et al., eds. (New York: Appleton Century, 1960), is a collection of twenty-odd essays on the comic and then a collection of examples. Paul Lauter, ed., *Theories of Comedy* (New York: Doubleday Anchor, 1969) is also an anthology.

For clowns, see Barbara Swain, *Fools and Folly During the Middle*

Ages and the Renaissance (New York: Columbia University Press, 1932); Enid Welsford, *The Fool: His Society and Literary History* (London: Faber & Faber, 1935; reissued in 1968); Erika Titze-Conrat, *Dwarfs and Jesters in Art* (London: Phaidon Press, 1957). See Samuel Miller's and Wolfgang Zucker's articles on the clown in *Theology Today*, 24, no. 3 (October 1967). Miller's is entitled "The Clown in Contemporary Art"; Zucker's is "The Clown as the Lord of Disorder."

Søren Kierkegaard was the first theological thinker in the modern period to say much about the comic, in his work on irony. In the English-speaking world, Gilbert Charles Chesterton provides a memorable example of the Christian comic élan. G. P. Fedotov includes a section on holy fools in the second volume of his *The Russian Mind* (Cambridge, Mass.: Harvard University Press, 1966), pp. 316–343. In an essay entitled "Sunday Masks and Pagan Faces," in *Religious Theatre*, 2 (Spring 1965), pp. 59–76, Marlow Hotchkiss examines the meaning of the slapstick and "grotesque clowning at the foot of the cross" in medieval comedy and rejects the notion that it was just simple-headed buffoonery. He contends that the medieval playwrights used comedy in part to express doubt and ambivalence about orthodox religious teaching. Also, he shows that even at such sacred moments as the nailing of Christ to the cross, the playwrights could not resist certain comic elements. In one part of the York cycle, for instance, the soldiers are embarrassed to discover that in preparing the cross they have bored the holes wrong, and Jesus' body will not fit.

Nathan A. Scott, Jr., has written a number of penetrating pieces on comedy. The best by far is "The Bias of Comedy and the Narrow Escape into Faith," first published in *The Christian Scholar*, 44 (Spring 1961). His most recent work in the theology of culture can be found in his collection of essays entitled *The Broken Center: Studies in the Theological Horizon of Modern Literature* (New Haven: Yale University Press, 1968) and in *The Modern Vision of Death* (Richmond: John Knox Press, 1967). Stanley Hopper explores irony in *The Crisis of Faith* (New York: Abingdon-Cokesbury Press, 1944). William Lynch, S.J., has a chapter on the comic in *Christ and Apollo* (New York: Sheed & Ward, 1960). Nelvin Vos has two books on the subject so far: *The Drama of Comedy* (Richmond: John Knox Press, 1966) and *For God's Sake Laugh* (Richmon: John Knox Press, 1967).

See also John Hunt, "Comic Escape and Anti-Vision: The Novels of Joseph Heller and Thomas Pynchon," and Preston M. Browning, Jr., "Flannery O'Connor and the Grotesque Recovery of the Holy," in Nathan A. Scott, Jr., ed., *Adversity and Grace* (Chicago: University of Chicago Press, 1968); David Grossvogel, "The Depths of Laughter: The Subsoil of a Culture," in *Yale French Studies,* 23 (Summer 1959), p. 66; Gunnar Urgang, "The Climate is the Comedy," in *The Christian Scholar,* 46 (Spring 1963), pp. 61–86; Ruth Nero, "Toward a Theory of Comedy," in *Journal of Aesthetics and Art Criticism,* 21 (Spring 1963), p. 328.

For the art of Corita Kent, see *Sister Corita* (Boston: Pilgrim Press, 1968), by Sister Corita Kent, Harvey Cox, and Samuel A. Eisenstein.

The German philosopher Eugen Fink published an analysis of the symbolic significance of play in 1960. It is entitled *Das Spiel als Weltsymbol* (Stuttgart: Kohlhammer, 1960). It succeeds an earlier work, *Oase des Glücks: Gedanken zu einer Ontologie des Spiels* (Freiburg: Alber, 1957). Fink argues, wrongly I think, that we are mistaken to set work and play in opposition to each other. He emphasizes what he calls the basic "ludic receptivity to being" and sees play and work as interpenetrating each other. I have argued, both in the chapter on festivity and in the section on play, that I think play *is* different from work. Their unity is not an ontological reality but a kind of eschatological hope. In so arguing I follow more closely the positions of Roger Caillois in *Les Jeux et les hommes* (Paris: Gallimard, 1958) and Johan Huizinga in *Homo Ludens* (Boston: Beacon Press, 1955). Jacques Ehrmann compares Caillois and Huizinga to Emile Benveniste whose essay "Le Jeu Comme Structure" (*Deucalion,* 2 [1947], pp. 161–167) I have not been able to examine. Ehrmann does so in an article beginning on p. 31 of a special issue of *Yale French Studies* entitled "Game, Play, Literature," available from Room 323, William Harkness Hall, Yale University, New Haven, Conn. 06520.

1. Günter Grass, *The Tin Drum,* Ralph Manheim, trans. (New York: Pantheon, 1963).

2. Henri Bergson, "Laughter," first written in 1900, reprinted in the John J. Enck et al. collection, pp. 43–64.

3. Maurice Bejart, as quoted in *Time,* December 15, 1967, p. 87.

4. Huizinga, *Homo Ludens.*

5. Romano Guardini, *The Spirit of the Liturgy,* Ada Lane, trans. (London: Sheed and Ward, 1930).

6. Sister Corita Kent, *Footnotes and Headlines: A Play and Pray Book* (New York: Herder and Herder, 1967).

7. Hugo Rahner, *Man at Play* (New York: Herder and Herder, 1967), p. 65.

8. Scott, *The Broken Center.*

9. Peter Berger, *The Precarious Vision* (New York: Doubleday, 1961).

10. Rahner, p. 21.

11. P. Lersch, *Die Philosophie des Humors,* as quoted in Rahner, p. 35.

12. Lawrence Durrell, *Clea* (New York: E. P. Dutton, 1960). See also Elton Trueblood, *The Humor of Christ* (New York: Harper, 1964).

13. Thornton Wilder, as quoted in Nelvin Vos, *The Drama of Comedy,* p. 30.

14. Wolfgang Zucker, "The Clown as the Lord of Disorder."

15. Joseph Heller, *Catch-22* (New York: Simon & Schuster, 1961).

16. R. W. B. Lewis, *Trials of the Word* (New Haven: Yale University Press, 1965), p. 212.

Appendix: Some Relevant Theological Currents

Husserl's main ideas can be found in the following English editions of his work: *Idea of Phenomenology* (New York: Humanities Press, n.d.), *Cartesian Meditations: An Introduction to Phenomenology* (New York: Humanities Press, 1960), and especially *Phenomenology and the Crisis of Philosophy* (New York: Harper, 1965).

William Lynch's best-known work is *Christ and Apollo* (New York: Sheed and Ward, 1960). A more recent work is *Images of Hope: Imagination as Healer of the Hopeless* (Baltimore: Helicon, 1965).

Tom Driver's work has appeared mainly in essays, but his *The Sense of History in Greek and Shakespearean Drama* (New York: Columbia University Press, 1960) is fundamental.

For Walter Ong, S.J., see *The Barbarian Within* (New York: Macmillan, 1962), *In the Human Grain* (New York: Macmillan, 1967), and *The Presence of the Word* (New Haven: Yale University Press, 1967).

Maynard Kaufman has an essay in a volume edited by Nathan Scott entitled *Adversity and Grace: Studies in Recent American Literature* (volume 4 of *Essays in Divinity,* Chicago: University of Chicago Press, 1968). He also has an essay entitled "Post-Christian Aspects of the New Theology" in T. J. J. Altizer, ed., *Toward a New Christianity* (New York: Harcourt, Brace, 1968).

1. Karl Barth, *Epistle to the Romans,* Edwyn C. Hoskyns, trans. (New York: Oxford University Press, 1963).

2. Leslie Dewart, *The Future of Belief* (New York: Herder and Herder, 1966); *The Foundations of Belief* (New York: Herder and Herder, 1969).

3. Gregory Baum, *Faith and Doctrine* (Toronto: Paulist Newman Press, 1969).

4. Richard R. Niebuhr, *Schleiermacher: On Christ and Religion* (New York: Scribner, 1964).

5. Paul Lehmann, *Ethics in a Christian Context* (New York: Harper, 1963).

6. Scott, *The Broken Center.*

7. See above for references to Kaufman, Lynch, Driver, and Ong.

8. Maurice Merleau-Ponty, *Phenomenology of Perception,* C. Smith, trans. (New York: Humanities Press, 1962).

9. Robert Bellah, "Civil Religion in America," *Daedalus,* 96, no. 1 (Winter 1967), pp. 1–22.

10. Peter Berger, *A Rumour of Angels* (New York: Doubleday, 1969).

11. Thomas Luckmann, *The Invisible Religion* (New York: Macmillan, 1967).

Index of Names

Index of Names